ETERNAL
ECHOES

LA Tribune Publishing

The Right of Muriel Blanc to be identified as the
Author of the work has been asserted by her in accordance
with the Copyright Act 1988.

LA Tribune Publishing
name has been established by LA Tribune.

All Rights Reserved.

No part of this publication may be reproduced, distributed, or transmitted in any form or by any means, including photocopying, recording, or other electronic or mechanical methods without the prior and express written permission of the author or publisher, except in the case of brief quotations embodied in critical reviews and certain other noncommercial uses permitted by copyright law.

Printed in the United States of America
ISBN- 9798869167590
Copyright@2024 Muriel Blanc

ETERNAL ECHOES

The alchemy of resilience after losing someone to cancer

By
MURIEL BLANC

ABOUT THE AUTHOR

Eternal echoes" the alchemy of resilience after losing someone to cancer.

For over three decades, Muriel has stood as a beacon of hope, a transformative force guiding individuals through profound change. Her journey, marked by many setbacks, including the poignant grief of losing her husband to cancer, infuses her work with a depth that resonates with those navigating similar paths. Recognized by the Los Angeles Tribune for "The Art of Healing from Trauma to Transformation," Muriel has become synonymous with words like "gifted healer" and "guiding light," leaving an extraordinary impact on all touched by her influence.

With an alchemical blend of compassion, empathy, and intuition, Muriel has facilitated from all walks of life countless individuals' transformative journeys. Her focus on the 12 universal laws and alchemy forms the foundation for unlocking true selves, igniting potential, and manifesting lives abundantly in love and well-being.

In her nurturing space, Muriel empowers clients to challenge self-limiting beliefs, replacing them with aspirations aligned with their true goals. Drawing from diverse modalities like Energetic Inner Child work, shamanic practices, reiki, sound healing, and color therapy, she crafts a toolkit that resonates with the unique needs of each individual.

Muriel's intuitive connection delves into the depths of souls, illuminating hidden patterns and transforming vulnerability into strength. In her new book, "Eternal Echoes: Alchemy of Resilience After Losing Someone to Cancer." draws on a wealth of experience in guiding individuals through the challenges of trauma. Muriel's unique approach empowers individuals to not only navigate pain but also transform it into profound growth and resilience. Through coaching techniques, mindfulness practices, and personalized strategies, Muriel becomes a supportive guide on a transformative journey of self-discovery, helping clients unearth their inner strength.

Through transformative techniques, Muriel guides her clients to recalibrate their emotional, mental, physical, and energy bodies. The outcomes are profound: self-love blossoms, acceptance replaces self-criticism, trust in the universe takes root, and the need for control surrenders to life's unfolding journey.

At the core of Muriel's mission is a simple yet profound belief: every individual is inherently whole and complete, an integral thread in the fabric of the universe. Unwavering in her commitment, she nurtures this belief within her clients, guiding them to trust their internal compass and pursue their dreams with unwavering faith.

For those ready for profound change, Muriel invites them to embrace the transformative power of her coaching and healing. Together, they unlock latent potential, transmuting life's challenges, including the poignant grief of loss, into the purest gold of self-realization, joy, and fulfillment.

FOREWORD

Foreword by Moe Rock, CEO LA Tribune

It is with profound honor and a deep sense of gratitude that I write this foreword for Muriel Blanc's extraordinary book. Having the privilege to work alongside Muriel, to witness her journey from up close, and to be a part of the team that brought her powerful story to publication, has been one of the most impactful experiences of my life.

Muriel's work is not just a book; it is a beacon of resilience and strength, a guide through life's most turbulent storms. Her story, though rooted in personal tragedy, transcends the individual experience and speaks to the universal human condition. In her vivid narrative, Muriel captures the essence of what it means to confront the unthinkable, to navigate the depths of sorrow, and to emerge with a newfound understanding of life's fragile beauty.

The introduction of her book offers a glimpse into the day that changed everything. Muriel's recounting of a seemingly ordinary moment, shattered by a sudden health crisis, is both heart wrenching and beautifully poignant. Her words paint a picture so vivid, it is as if we are in the room with her, experiencing the confusion and fear that enveloped her family.

However, this book is more than a story of loss and despair. It is a testament to the strength of the human spirit. Muriel's

Foreword

journey, from the shock of her husband's diagnosis to the transformative path she embarked upon, is a powerful reminder of our capacity for resilience. Her background as a transformational coach, artist, writer, and Reiki Master adds a unique depth to her insights, making her story a compelling guide for anyone facing life's challenges.

What makes Muriel's narrative profoundly impactful is its universality. While the specifics of her experience are unique, the lessons she imparts are relevant to us all. This book is an invaluable resource for anyone grappling with adversity. It offers hope, not through platitudes or wishful thinking, but through the honest and raw recounting of a journey through life's most challenging moments.

As you turn the pages of Muriel's book, you will embark on a journey that is both deeply personal and universally relevant. You will find not only a story of loss and pain but also a roadmap for finding strength in vulnerability, for transforming suffering into wisdom, and for discovering the resilience that lies within each of us.

I am immensely proud to have played a role in bringing Muriel's powerful message to the world. Her book is a gift, a source of strength and resilience that is needed now more than ever. I invite you to delve into these pages, to immerse yourself in Muriel's journey, and to discover the profound lessons of resilience that she so eloquently shares.

This is more than just a book; it is a companion for anyone navigating the complexities of life. Muriel Blanc has offered us a rare glimpse into the depths of the human heart, and for that, we are eternally grateful.

DEDICATED

In loving memory of my late Husband who died of terminal cancer on November 29, 2018

Extreme gratitude to my three children Allyson, Samantha, and William who were and are my pillar of strength.

TABLE OF CONTENTS

About The Author iv
Foreword vi
Dedicated viii
Introduction 1
Chapter 1: The Alchemy of Resilience 8
Chapter 2: Facing the Darkness of Loss 17
Chapter 3: Navigating the Alchemical Process 25
Chapter 4: Finding Light Amidst Darkness 46
Chapter 5: Building a Supportive Network 55
Chapter 6: Healing Power of a Positive Mindset 67
Chapter 7: Embracing Healing Modalities 78
Chapter 8: The Universal Laws of Healing 85
Chapter 9: Honoring the Eternal Echoes 95
Chapter 10: Creating a new Vision 108
Epilogue: Embracing the Eternal Echoes
of Love and Resilience 117
Further Reading and Supportive Resources 119

Introduction

During an ordinary day, our lives were irrevocably altered. The sun inundated the world in the soft, golden light of a spring midday. I can still recall the way the sunlight danced through the sunroom's windows lighting the dining room and casting intricate patterns on the table. My husband was in the middle of a sentence when it happened.

He was animatedly discussing one of his favorite topics on astrology, his voice filled with passion and enthusiasm. We shared a meal as a family, a simple yet cherished routine in our lives. The aroma of freshly brewed coffee lingered in the air, intermingling with the soft clinking of cutlery against porcelain plates. It was a scene of normalcy, a snapshot of happiness that would soon be shattered.

Suddenly, my husband's words faltered. His expression shifted from animated to confused, then to one of silent desperation. He clutched his throat as if he had been robbed of his voice. It was as if his very words had been stolen away, leaving him in a realm of silence. Time itself seemed to stretch, and those agonizing seconds felt like an eternity.

The room suddenly filled with a palpable sense of dread. My son and I exchanged worried, bewildered glances; our concern mirrored in each other's eyes. We reached out to him, but our hands were unsteady. He looked at us, his eyes pleading for understanding as he struggled to communicate his distress. All around us, the world continued to spin, blissfully unaware of the turmoil within those four walls.

And then, as abruptly as it had begun, the ordeal ended. My husband's voice returned, but his strength seemed to wane. He attempted to stand, his movements slow and shaky, and it was as if the ground beneath him had become unsteady. The realization that something was terribly wrong dawned upon us.

Without hesitation, my son and I acted in unison, driven by an instinct that only surfaces in moments of crisis. We helped my husband to his feet, our hands supporting his trembling body. Each step was a monumental effort, and he teetered as if the earth itself were no longer a stable foundation. Our voices were calm on the surface, but beneath that facade was a torrent of distress and confusion.

As we carefully guided him towards the car, my thoughts were racing. What was happening to the man I loved? What had caused this sudden and inexplicable loss of speech and motor control? Did he have a seizure or a mini-stroke? I tried to reassure myself on our way to the Emergency Room and kept telling myself that doctors would surely provide answers and solutions that would be an easy fix, but deep down, I knew that our lives were about to take a tumultuous turn.

It was a sunny spring morning, a time when life should have been blooming with new beginnings and vibrant hope. Instead, it marked the beginning of a journey into the unknown, a journey that would test the very beliefs I had held dear throughout my life.

As a transformational coach, my world was centered on the principles of positivity, healing, and spiritual growth. I have delved into the laws of the universe, exploring their profound influence on our lives. I had written and spoken passionately about the remarkable ability of the human spirit to heal and

Introduction

transform. My words had been a beacon of hope for those seeking to mend their hearts and find their inner strength.

Yet, at this moment, I was confronted with a reality that no amount of positive thinking or manifestation could have prepared me for. The ER started to run test after test and moved him to a private room. The Neurosurgeon's words still echo in my mind: "Your husband's brain tumor is inoperable, if we operate, he will be a vegetable." The hope and dreams that once resided in that voice had given way to the weight of an insurmountable burden.

As I absorbed this devastating news, the room around me seemed to constrict, as if mirroring the suffocating alarm that had taken hold of my heart. The walls closed in, and for a brief, surreal instant, I felt as though the universe itself had shifted to accommodate this new, heart-wrenching reality.

In that moment, time stood still, and I was thrust into a world I had never imagined entering. The vast expanse of my spiritual and intellectual understanding seemed inadequate to navigate the overwhelming feeling of helplessness that had washed over me. The challenge that lay ahead was unlike any I had ever faced, and it tested the very core of my beliefs and the resilience of my spirit.

The path that stretched before me was a treacherous one, paved with uncertainty and heartache. I would soon learn that the journey through the impending loss of the man I had been for 3 years who was my confidant and greatest supporter, would require a strength I had yet to discover within myself. It was a path that would redefine my understanding of healing, resilience, and the enduring power of the human spirit.

It was in the wake of this life-altering diagnosis that I realized the profound irony of my own journey. As an artist, writer, and Reiki Master, I had dedicated my life to exploring the mystical, the unseen, and the boundless potential that resided within every individual. The very essence of my work had been to empower people, encouraging them to tap into their inner reservoirs of strength and healing. And yet, here I was, on the precipice of a profound transformation I could never have foreseen.

In the days that followed that fateful diagnostic, our lives became a whirlwind of medical appointments, consultations, and tests. The hospital waiting rooms became a hauntingly familiar backdrop to our existence, and the sterile scent of antiseptic clung to our clothes like an unwelcome companion. We met doctors who delivered prognoses and statistics that felt more like a prison sentence than a path to recovery.

It was in those moments, as I sat beside my husband in those sterile rooms, that I found myself reaching deep into my reservoir of knowledge and understanding. The principles of Reiki and intuitive coaching became more than just concepts; they became lifelines. I channeled my inner energy, offering love and healing to my husband and myself, and I guided my son in doing the same.

We learned to communicate in silence, our eyes and gestures conveying what words could not. It was a communication born of love, shared experiences, and a deep connection that transcended the limitations of spoken language. In those moments, I discovered the true meaning of intuitive coaching - the ability to listen to the unspoken words of the heart.

As I navigated the labyrinthine corridors of the medical world, I also found solace in my writing. My notebooks became my sanctuary, a place where I could pour my emotions, fears, and hopes into words. Each pen stroke was a prayer, each page a testament to the resilience of the human spirit. My writing was no longer a form of expression; it was a form of catharsis, a lifeline that helped me maintain my own sanity in the face of overwhelming uncertainty.

Introduction

I often thought about the books I had read and my studies, the ones that explored the magic of healing and the strength of the human spirit. The words of Wayne Dyer, Gregg Braden, and other luminaries echoed in my mind. They had spoken of the power of positive thinking, of the ability to shape our reality through intention and belief. But could these principles hold true in the darkest of times, in the shadow of an inoperable brain tumor?

I realized that the answer was not a simple "yes" or "no." Instead, it was a complex tapestry of emotions, beliefs, and actions. It was about finding the balance between hope and acceptance, between visualization and surrender. It was about acknowledging the harsh reality of the present while still holding space for the possibility of miracles.

In the pages of my own life, I rewrote the script. I became not only the author but also the protagonist of a story I had never envisioned. The narrative shifted from one of empowerment and healing to one of resilience and surrender. It was a story of learning to embrace the unknown, to find strength in vulnerability, and to discover the alchemy of the human spirit.

The path was not linear, and it was filled with moments of despair and doubt. There were nights when tears flowed freely and when the weight of the future felt unbearable. But there were also moments of profound connection and love when the simple act of holding hands became a source of solace and strength.

As I reflect on this journey, I am reminded of the words of Wayne Dyer: "With everything that has happened to you, you can either feel sorry for yourself or treat what has happened as a gift. Everything is either an opportunity to grow or an obstacle to keep you from growing. You get to choose." These words became my mantra, my guiding light in the darkest hours.

I came to understand that resilience was not about denying the pain or putting on a facade of strength. It was about acknowledging the pain, the fear, and the uncertainty and still finding the courage to move forward. It was about surrendering to the unknown and finding grace in vulnerability.

In the chapters that followed, I will take you on this journey of resilience, a journey that was born from the crucible of loss and transformed into a testament to the enduring power of the human spirit. It is a journey that defies easy categorization, one that weaves together the threads of hope, despair, love, and acceptance. It is a journey that is deeply personal yet universal, for it is a journey that we all undertake in one form or another.

As we explore the alchemy of resilience, we will delve into the lessons learned, the wisdom gained, and the transformation that occurs when we embrace the full spectrum of human experience. We will navigate the challenges of caregiving, the complexities of medical decisions, and the emotional rollercoaster that comes with a life-altering diagnosis. We will uncover the healing power of art and writing, the depth of intuitive coaching, and the transformative potential of the human heart.

But most importantly, we will embark on a journey of the spirit, one that transcends the limitations of the physical world. We will discover that even in the face of the darkest storms, the human spirit has the capacity to find light, to unearth the eternal echoes of hope and resilience that reside within us all.

This is not just a book; it is a testament to the human spirit's remarkable capacity to transcend adversity and find meaning in the most challenging of circumstances. It is a story of love, loss, and the enduring legacy of the human heart. It is a journey that invites you to embrace your own resilience and discover the alchemy that resides within you.

Introduction

Join me as we explore the depths of the human spirit and uncover the eternal echoes of hope and healing. The journey is just beginning, and the pages of this book are an open invitation to embark on a life-changing exploration of the alchemy of resilience.

CHAPTER 1

The Alchemy of Resilience

Our journey begins with the recognition that life is a tapestry woven from moments of both light and shadow. It is in the shadowed corners of existence that we often find our greatest opportunities for growth and transformation. It was in one such shadowed corner that I discovered the true essence of resilience.

As I stood at the threshold of uncertainty, with the weight of my husband's diagnosis heavy on my shoulders, I realized that the path we were treading was not one of despair, but rather an alchemical journey. The word "alchemy" is often associated with the transmutation of base metals into gold, a symbol of transformation and transcendence. In our case, it was not metal but the human spirit that would undergo a profound transformation.

Alchemy, often associated with the transformation of base metals into gold, finds a profound metaphorical resonance in the context of grief and loss. In this emotional crucible, the human spirit is tested, and the process of alchemy becomes a guiding light, illuminating the transformative potential that lies within the depths of our suffering.

In the alchemical context of grief, transformation is not a mere wish or aspiration; it's a necessity. Just as alchemists sought to transmute base elements into precious gold, individuals grappling with loss must transmute their pain and suffering into a source of healing, growth, and resilience. This metaphorical alchemical process is a testimony to the enduring power of the human spirit.

The journey of alchemical transformation in the face of grief begins with the acknowledgment that life has irrevocably changed. The loss of a loved one is a crucible that shatters the old reality, leaving fragments of memories and emotions. Like the alchemist's crucible, this moment of profound sorrow is where the true work of transformation begins.

Just as the alchemist carefully combines and heats the elements within the crucible, the grieving individual must navigate the complex mixture of emotions that arises. Denial, anger, bargaining, depression, and acceptance - these emotional phases become the elements that must be understood and transformed.

Resilience, within this metaphor, is the fire that heats the crucible. It's the internal strength that propels the individual to confront their grief head-on, to feel the pain deeply, and to engage with the emotions without flinching. It's the choice to acknowledge that this process is essential for transformation, much like how fire is necessary for alchemical transmutation.

The alchemical journey through grief is also about seeking the philosopher's stone, the elusive substance that grants eternal life and wisdom. In the context of loss, this philosopher's stone symbolizes the wisdom and growth that can be gleaned from the experience. It's the recognition that the journey through grief can lead to a deeper understanding of life's impermanence, the value of love and connection, and the strength of the human spirit.

As the alchemical process unfolds, individuals often find themselves questioning their beliefs and values. This is akin to the process of calcination in traditional alchemy, where base metals are reduced to ashes. In the realm of grief and loss, calcination represents the breakdown of old beliefs and the need to reevaluate one's understanding of life and death.

The process of alchemical sublimation, where matter is transformed from solid to gas without an intermediate liquid state, mirrors the ethereal nature of memory and connection in the face of loss. The memories of a loved one take on an almost otherworldly quality, transcending the physical realm and becoming a source of solace and inspiration.

The final stage of alchemical transformation, known as conjunction, represents the unification of opposites, the merging of the conscious and unconscious. In grief, this represents the synthesis of pain and healing, of despair and hope. It's the recognition that these seemingly opposing forces can coexist, and that grief can be a wellspring of resilience and growth.

Ultimately, the alchemical metaphor in the context of grief and loss is a reminder that even in the darkest of moments, there is the potential for transformation and growth. It's a testament to the human spirit's remarkable capacity to transmute suffering into strength, to find meaning in the depths of sorrow, and to embrace the eternal echoes of love and connection.

In the crucible of grief, the alchemical process is not one of creating gold; it is the creation of a soul that has been tempered and refined by the fire of loss, a soul that emerges with a greater capacity for compassion, empathy, and resilience. It is the understanding that, like the alchemist's quest for the philosopher's stone, the journey through grief can yield wisdom, healing, and the enduring legacy of love.

The journey of resilience is not about avoiding suffering or erasing the pain of loss, for that is an impossibility in human experience. Instead, it is about finding meaning in the midst of suffering, about discovering the golden threads that run through the fabric of our pain. It is a journey of healing, not in the sense of erasing our wounds, but in the sense of finding strength and wisdom in their presence. Resilience doesn't mean that the pain disappears; it means that it is met with courage and transformed into a source of strength.

Resilience, often celebrated as an emblem of strength and adaptability, takes on a unique and profound meaning in the context of grief and loss. In the face of profound sorrow, it becomes a beacon of hope, a path to healing, and a testament to the indomitable nature of the human spirit.

Resilience in grief is about facing the brutal reality of loss while refusing to surrender to despair. It is the capacity to navigate the storm of emotions, from anger and denial to bargaining and acceptance, and find one's way through the tempest. It's the strength to grieve without judgment, allowing each emotion to wash over like waves, knowing that healing requires the release of pent-up feelings.

Resilience is the choice to move forward, even when the path is obscured by the weight of grief. It is about taking one step at a time, even if those steps are hesitant and faltering. It's acknowledging that, at times, resilience may mean simply getting out of bed in the morning, or it may manifest as the determination to face each day, despite the ache that lingers in one's heart.

Resilience is the ability to bounce back from adversity, to adapt to change, and to grow stronger in the face of challenges. Losing a loved one to cancer is an incredibly painful experience that can shake us to our core. However, it is in these moments of profound grief that resilience can emerge. It is a coping mechanism that can help us find a new sense of purpose and meaning in life, despite the immense loss we have endured.

In the context of grief, resilience is intrinsically tied to acceptance. It's the recognition that the world has changed, that a loved one is no longer physically present, and that the future is different from what was once imagined. It's the capacity to redefine one's identity in a world that has been reshaped by loss, to reestablish a sense of purpose, and to embark on a journey of self-discovery in the aftermath of heartbreak.

Resilience is about seeking support, whether from friends, family, or professionals. It's the acknowledgment that no one needs to bear the burden of grief alone. In seeking help, resilience manifests as a willingness to share the pain, to communicate one's needs, and to hold space for one's own healing.

In the face of grief, resilience also encompasses the ability to find meaning and purpose. It's the transformation of pain into a source of inspiration, a catalyst for personal growth. It's using the experience of loss to become a more compassionate, empathetic, and understanding individual. It's recognizing the preciousness of life and the value of every moment.

Ultimately, resilience in the context of grief and loss is about acknowledging the presence of pain while seeking the potential for growth and transformation. It's a testament to the human spirit's enduring capacity to find beauty in the midst of suffering, and just like the mystical phoenix to rise from the ashes of sorrow, and to discover hope in the eternal echoes of love and connection.

In the realm of grief and loss, we often find extraordinary stories of individuals who have demonstrated remarkable resilience after losing loved ones to cancer. These real-life examples serve as shining beacons of hope, illustrating the profound capacity of the human spirit to rise, find purpose, and inspire others in the wake of devastating loss. Let's delve into the stories of a few such remarkable individuals who have faced the weight of cancer's impact with unwavering strength and grace:"

1. **Randy Pausch - "The Last Lecture":** Randy Pausch was a computer science professor diagnosed with terminal pancreatic cancer. After his diagnosis, he gave a moving and inspirational lecture known as "The Last Lecture" at Carnegie Mellon University. Pausch's resilience in the face of his illness, as well as his wisdom and humor, left a lasting impact on those who heard his lecture and read his book, which was also titled "The Last Lecture."
2. **Elizabeth Edwards - Advocacy for Cancer Research:** Elizabeth Edwards, the late wife of former U.S. Senator John Edwards, faced a breast cancer diagnosis. Despite her own struggles with the disease, she used her experience to advocate for cancer research and raise awareness about the importance of early detection. Her resilience in the face of cancer not only inspired others but also contributed to meaningful changes in healthcare policy.
3. **Stuart Scott - An ESPN Icon's Fight:** Stuart Scott, a beloved ESPN anchor, fought a long battle with cancer before his passing. Throughout his journey, he demonstrated incredible resilience, continuing to work and inspiring countless individuals with his courageous fight against the disease. His catchphrases and positive attitude endeared him to viewers, and his legacy lives on in the sports broadcasting world.
4. **Dr. Paul Kalanithi - "When Breath Becomes Air":** Dr. Paul Kalanithi was a neurosurgeon who authored the memoir "When Breath Becomes Air." He wrote this moving book while facing a terminal lung cancer diagnosis. His story of resilience and the exploration of life and death touched the hearts of readers worldwide. Dr. Kalanithi's determination to find meaning in the face of death serves as an enduring testament to the human spirit.

5. **Jill Costello - Rowing for Cancer Awareness:** Jill Costello was a college rower diagnosed with lung cancer at a young age. Despite her illness, she continued to pursue her passion for rowing and used her platform to raise awareness about lung cancer. Her resilience and advocacy inspired those around her and highlighted the importance of early cancer detection.

Lastly, resilience has a profound impact on our overall health and wellness. When we develop resilience, we become better equipped to manage stress, maintain healthy relationships, and make positive lifestyle choices. It enables us to prioritize self-care, both physically and emotionally, leading to improved overall well-being. By understanding and embracing resilience, we can transform our journey of grief and loss into an opportunity for personal growth and healing.

This transformation is exemplified by stories of individuals who have faced profound adversity and turned their pain into purpose. These inspiring figures prove that even in the face of the darkest trials, the human spirit can rise, find meaning, and create positive change. Their stories serve as beacons of hope, reminding us that resilience is not only a theoretical concept but a tangible force for transformation and healing. The individuals below are just a few of the many who have faced diverse forms of suffering and hardship, yet they all found a way to turn their pain into a greater purpose. Their stories serve as powerful examples of how resilience, determination, and a commitment to making the world a better place can arise from the depths of adversity.

1. **Victor Frankl - Finding Meaning in Suffering:** Victor Frankl, a Holocaust survivor, endured unimaginable

suffering in concentration camps during World War II. Despite the horrors he faced, Frankl found a sense of purpose by developing logotherapy, a psychotherapeutic approach that focuses on finding meaning in all forms of existence, even in the midst of intense suffering. His book "Man's Search for Meaning" has since inspired countless individuals to find purpose in their own adversities.

2. **Malala Yousafzai - Empowering Through Education:** Malala Yousafzai, a Pakistani advocate for girls' education, was shot by the Taliban for attending school. Rather than succumbing to fear, she transformed her pain into a global movement for girls' education. Malala's bravery and her work through the Malala Fund have empowered girls worldwide; reminding us all that one person's resilience can ignite change.

3. **Nelson Mandela - Forgiveness and Reconciliation:** Nelson Mandela, who spent 27 years in prison during South Africa's apartheid era, emerged not with bitterness but with a commitment to reconciliation and forgiveness. He became South Africa's first black president and worked tirelessly to dismantle apartheid and bring healing to a divided nation. Mandela's story is a testament to the power of forgiveness and transformation.

4. **Liz Murray - From Homeless to Harvard:** Liz Murray's story is one of remarkable resilience. She grew up in extreme poverty, often homeless, and lost her mother to AIDS. Yet, through her determination and education, she transformed her life. Murray went from living on the streets to graduating from Harvard University, and she now advocates for the education of homeless youth.

5. **Nick Vujicic - Overcoming Physical Limitations:** Nick Vujicic was born without limbs, facing a life filled with physical challenges and emotional pain. He has since become a motivational speaker, author, and advocate for people with disabilities. Nick's story is a testament to the power of self-acceptance and using one's difficulties to inspire others to overcome their obstacles.

CHAPTER 2

Facing the Darkness of Loss

Delving into the raw emotions and challenges accompanying the loss of a loved one to cancer is an essential step toward understanding the profound impact of this experience. It's about acknowledging the depth and complexity of grief, the weight of helplessness, and the multitude of emotions that arise. It's also about finding ways to navigate these challenges, heal, and eventually transform the journey of loss into an opportunity for personal growth and healing.

The journey of losing a loved one to cancer is a profound and life-altering experience. The grief that follows is as unique as a fingerprint, different for each individual.

Grief is a natural response to loss, a language of the soul, and it's crucial to remember that there is no 'right' or 'wrong' way to grieve. It's an intensely personal voyage, a solitary walk through the labyrinth of emotions, and everyone forges their path differently. However, by embarking on this journey of understanding the grief process, we may find threads of wisdom that can guide us toward healing and the emergence of our inner resilience.

One of the initial stages of this profound journey is shock and denial. When we first experience the absence of our spouse, the mind often grapples with the incredulity of reality. This phase may wrap us in a cocoon of numbness and disbelief. Recognizing that these initial reactions are not only normal but also a part of the profound journey can be the first step towards embracing our emotions and inching forward.

As we traverse the labyrinth of grief, we may stumble upon intense emotions such as anger, guilt, and sadness. These emotions can resemble storms, overwhelming and tempestuous. Acknowledging them, inviting them into our conscious world, is a vital part of healing alchemy. We must grant ourselves the permission to grieve, to allow these emotions to unfurl, for it is in feeling deep that we eventually find the path to solace.

Within the complex labyrinth of grief, there lies a realm of self-care. Engaging in nurturing activities, be it through the dance of exercise, the stillness of meditation, or the whispered confidences of journaling, can be like a soothing balm for the soul. It's in these gentle self-indulgences that we catch glimpses of healing and the promise of a rekindled spirit. Seeking the embrace of others who have tread similar paths, or finding solace in support groups where we can weave our stories into a collective tapestry of strength, is an essential thread in this labyrinthine journey.

Throughout the labyrinthine journey of grief, it becomes imperative to nurture our emotional intelligence and self-awareness. As we recognize and come to terms with the ebb and flow of our emotions, we gain a surer footing within this emotional terrain. But it's not just recognition; self-belief takes center stage as a cornerstone of resilience during this trying odyssey. It is the cultivation of a sunlit perspective, a steadfast belief in our capacity to mend and evolve, that significantly contributes to our overall well-being.

In closing, the journey through grief is a formidable path that every individual who has lost a spouse to cancer must traverse. By embarking on an exploration of the intricate stages of grief, by giving voice to our emotions, and by seeking out healthy avenues for solace, we commence the delicate process of healing and the construction of our internal fortitude. Developing emotional intelligence, fostering self-awareness, and nurturing a positive mindset is akin to forging a lantern to guide us through the labyrinth. It's within these tools that we unearth the inner strength to step forward and embrace life once more. Remember, you are never alone in this journey, and there is always a beacon of hope illuminating a path to a brighter tomorrow.

Acknowledging the Truth of the Loss

Losing a loved one to cancer is undeniably one of life's most formidable trials. The anguish, sorrow, and overwhelming surge of emotions often make it arduous to confront the harsh reality of the loss. Nevertheless, acknowledging this painful truth is a pivotal step on the path to recovery and the reconstruction of your life.

Accepting the reality of the loss doesn't equate to forgetting or moving on from the cherished memories of your beloved spouse. It signifies the recognition that they are no longer physically present, and your life has taken an unforeseen turn. This acknowledgment is a process often fraught with difficulty. It is natural to experience a spectrum of emotions, from denial and anger to sadness and confusion. However, comprehending that these emotions are an integral part of the grieving journey can provide guidance as you navigate through them.

Embracing personal development assumes paramount importance during this challenging phase. By accepting the reality of the loss, you open doors to possibilities of growth and self-discovery. This loss can serve as a catalyst for personal transformation. It offers you the opportunity to reassess your priorities, unveil your inner fortitude, and redefine your identity. Embracing personal development can help you discover purpose and meaning in life, even in the wake of profound loss.

Fostering a positive mindset and self-belief is indispensable for progress after losing a spouse to cancer. Acknowledging the truth of the loss empowers you to shift your perspective and concentrate on the positive aspects of your life. It enables you to find gratitude in the memories you've shared with your spouse and the love that endures within you. By nurturing a positive mindset, you gain the strength to surmount challenges and seize new opportunities.

The roles of emotional intelligence and self-awareness are pivotal in the process of recognizing the reality of the loss. These faculties encompass the comprehension and management of your emotions, the identification of triggers that may intensify your grief, and the practice of self-care. Developing emotional intelligence and self-awareness equips you with the tools to navigate the tumultuous seas of grief with compassion, both for others and for yourself. It allows you to honor your emotions while gradually embracing the truth of the loss.

Acknowledging the reality of the loss is a deeply personal and transformative odyssey. It necessitates time, patience, and self-compassion. By recognizing the pain and sorrow, you embark on a journey of personal growth, the cultivation of a positive perspective, and the nurturing of emotional intelligence and self-awareness. Remember, you are never alone on this expedition. Reach out to supportive communities, seek professional assistance, and surround yourself with loved ones who can offer solace and understanding. Together, we can unearth the strength to rebuild our lives and pay homage to the cherished memories of our beloved spouses.

Traversing the Phases of Grief

The loss of losing someone close to cancer is an undoubtedly soul-shattering experience. The emotions that surge within, coupled with the profound sense of emptiness, can feel like an unbearable weight, pressing down on the very core of your being. Nevertheless, navigating the phases of grief offers a path to healing and the reconstruction of a positive outlook after such a profound loss.

The initial stage of grief often unfolds as a denial. It is entirely natural to grapple with the impossibility of accepting the reality of your spouse's passing, especially when the pain is freshly etched in your heart. Denial acts as a gentle guardian, a veil that allows you to slowly come to terms with the heart-wrenching truth and adjust to your altered reality. Acknowledging your denial and permitting yourself to grieve at your own rhythm is a vital step.

As the cloak of denial gradually lifts, you may find yourself traversing into the realm of anger. Feelings of anger, whether directed at your spouse, the healthcare system, or even yourself, can rise to the surface. It's imperative to recognize that anger is an inherent part of the grieving process. Yet, it is equally crucial to uncover constructive outlets for this potent emotion. Engaging in physical activities or leaning on the support of cherished ones can serve as conduits to channel your anger constructively.

Next, the stage of bargaining comes into view. Here, you may find yourself negotiating with a higher power, yearning for a miracle, or wishing that circumstances could have unfolded differently. It's essential to acknowledge these thoughts and comprehend that they form an integral part of the journey towards healing. While pondering what might have been is natural, it is vital to seek ways to release the burden of guilt that often accompanies this phase.

Depression is another challenging facet of grief. The profound sadness and the void it carves can be overwhelming at times. In these moments, it is imperative to remember that seeking professional assistance or connecting with support groups can provide the crucial emotional support needed to traverse through this stage. Surrounding yourself with individuals who understand and empathize can guide you through the depths of depression, offering glimmers of hope amidst the shadowed valleys.

Finally, acceptance beckons as the stage where you begin to make peace with your loss and set the foundation for rebuilding your life. It is essential to comprehend that acceptance does not translate to forgetting your loved one; rather, it signifies an embrace of the cherished memories and the discovery of a fresh sense of purpose. Celebrate the life shared with your spouse and permit yourself to envision a future brimming with fulfillment.

Traversing the phases of grief is an intimately personal voyage that unfolds at its own pace. By acknowledging and understanding these stages, you gradually assemble a positive outlook, nurture emotional intelligence, and cultivate self-awareness. Resilience, in its true essence, is not about erasing the pain but about unearthing inner strength in the face of adversity and constructing a new life, one illuminated by purpose and joy.

Embracing Transformation and Forging Ahead

The anguish of losing a spouse to cancer is a pain beyond words, leaving you adrift, overwhelmed, and uncertain about the path forward. Yet, within this formidable adversity, lies the potential to unearth inner strength and reconstruct a positive perspective.

Change is a constant companion in our journey through life. When we resist it, we inadvertently stifle our capacity for growth and healing. Instead, we must learn to greet change as a doorway to personal development. Each day, take small steps to challenge yourself, whether it's venturing into a new hobby, connecting with new souls, or championing a fresh cause. By venturing beyond the boundaries of your comfort zone, you unlock a realm of uncharted experiences and prospects.

A positive mindset becomes your beacon as you traverse the intricate landscape of grief. It is essential to recall that while you may have lost your spouse, you have not lost yourself. Focus on nurturing a positive perspective by practicing gratitude, immersing yourself in the company of uplifting individuals, and engaging in activities that set your soul alight. Cultivate self-belief by recognizing your inherent strengths and capabilities reminding yourself that you are more than capable of conquering any challenges that come your way.

Emotional intelligence and self-awareness are steadfast companions in navigating the labyrinth of grief. Grant yourself permission to experience the full spectrum of emotions, both the uplifting and the somber, free from the burden of judgment. Acknowledge that the path of grief is a deeply individual journey for each person, and it's perfectly acceptable to take your time in the process of healing. Seek solace and understanding from the embrace of friends, family, or professional counselors who can offer guidance during this challenging juncture.

Reflect upon your emotions and reactions, and with each contemplation, fashion a profound understanding of yourself and your unique needs.

Moving forward does not entail forgetting your loved ones or diminishing their significance in your life. Instead, it is a tribute to their memory, living a life that's brimming with fulfillment and purpose. Dedicate time to rediscover your passions and dreams, and set new horizons and objectives. Remember that it's perfectly acceptable to have moments of despair, but steadfastly tread the path forward, one small step at a time, towards the promise of a brighter future.

In summary, embracing transformation and forging ahead after losing a spouse to cancer necessitates personal development, a buoyant perspective, emotional intelligence, and self-awareness. By actively participating in personal growth, nurturing a sunlit outlook on life, acknowledging and mastering your emotions, and setting fresh goals, you can progressively reconstruct your life and uncover renewed purpose and joy. Always keep in mind that resilience is not merely bouncing back; it's about bounding forward, emerging even stronger from the journey.

CHAPTER 3

Navigating the Alchemical Process

Navigating the Storm: Embracing and Mastering Your Emotions

The tempest that is losing someone to cancer is an ordeal that shakes the very foundations of our existence. It's like riding an emotional rollercoaster through the darkest of storms, leaving us drenched in feelings of loss, confusion, and sometimes even despair. However, within the heart of this maelstrom lies an opportunity to recognize and master these emotions, a crucial step on the path to healing and the construction of a resilient and positive mindset.

Grief, a tempestuous sea in itself, is our natural response to loss. It's a torrential rain of emotions - sadness, anger, guilt, relief - that we must allow ourselves to feel and express. These emotions, often conflicting and overwhelming, are the waves that crash upon the shores of our souls, reshaping the landscape of our inner world. The first step towards healing is in acknowledging and accepting this tumultuous sea of emotions, knowing that within its depths, we shall find our way to calmer waters.

Within this voyage of understanding and managing emotions, two guiding stars shine brightly: emotional intelligence and self-awareness. Emotional intelligence empowers you to not only identify and understand your own emotions but also to extend your empathy toward others who may be sailing through similar tempests. By honing this skill, you become better equipped to navigate the labyrinthine corridors of grief, forging resilience in the heart of adversity.

Self-awareness acts as the rudder in this tumultuous sea, helping you steer your emotional ship. Take time to reflect upon your feelings and chart the treacherous waters of your triggers. Knowing what intensifies your emotions allows you to harness this awareness, to be the master of your emotional responses. Seek refuge in the harbor of friends, family, or professionals versed in the art of grief counseling. Here, you shall find solace and understanding, a sanctuary where healing can begin.

Building a positive mindset upon this emotional terrain is a quest that requires self-belief and personal development. Never forget the incredible reservoir of strength and resilience that resides within you, a beacon of hope in the darkest of nights. Assemble around you the beacons of positivity, engage in activities that rekindle your spirit, that breathe life into your healing journey. It could be the camaraderie of support groups, the serenity of mindfulness and meditation, or the exploration of hobbies that whisper the secrets of personal growth.

In closing, remember that healing is not a sprint but a marathon, and your journey is as unique as a fingerprint. Grieve freely, give yourself the gift of patience in the face of emotional turbulence. Recognizing and managing your emotions is not about suppression; it's about embracing them as essential elements in your path to healing. By cultivating emotional intelligence, nurturing self-awareness, and forging a positive mindset, you shall navigate this tumultuous sea with the resilience and hope of a seasoned mariner.

Embracing Empathy and Nurturing Compassion

Losing a spouse or any loved one to cancer is a journey through a landscape of pain and despair, a path only those who have walked it can genuinely comprehend. It's like your world has crumbled, leaving you adrift, feeling alone and shattered. In these times of profound grief, the virtues of empathy and compassion emerge as guiding stars, essential companions on your odyssey of healing.

Empathy is the ability to not just comprehend but deeply share in the feelings of another person. It's a bridge that connects your heart to those who have weathered similar tempests, a conduit for mutual understanding and validation. By opening your heart to the pain of others, and by truly listening to their tales of loss, you create a haven of healing and solace. Surrounding yourself with those who can empathize with your journey lifts your spirits, reminding you that you're not alone in your quest.

Compassion walks hand in hand with empathy, translating understanding into action aimed at alleviating suffering. It manifests as acts of kindness, as a wellspring of understanding and support. In extending compassion to yourself, you unlock the doors to self-care and self-love, two indispensable keys to the healing process. You deserve the gentle touch of kindness during these trying times, a recognition of your pain, and permission to heal at your own pace.

The development of empathy and compassion requires a conscious endeavor to nurture a positive mindset and self-belief. Recognize that grief is a complex and intensely individual journey, a swirling tapestry of emotions. Grant yourself the gift of grieving, and in this grieving, be gentle and patient with your spirit. Embrace self-compassion by indulging in activities that kindle your joy and provide solace, whether it's communing with nature, capturing your thoughts in a journal, or seeking the guidance of professional therapy.

Emotional intelligence and self-awareness, our trusted companions, have vital roles to play in the cultivation of empathy and compassion. Carve out moments to contemplate your own emotions and experiences, allowing yourself to journey through them fully. In this profound self-awareness, you shall find the wellspring from which empathy flows deeper, for understanding your own complexities equips you to delve into the complexities of others.

In closing, developing empathy and compassion after the loss of a loved one to cancer is a beacon of hope on your healing journey. As you connect with those who have walked similar paths and extend the gentle hand of kindness to your own soul, you weave a web of support and love. Remember to be patient, to embrace self-compassion, and to nurture emotional intelligence. Through these practices, you shall construct a positive mindset and a spirit of resilience to guide you toward the radiant dawn of a new day.

Navigating the Depths of Self-Awareness and Emotion Mastery

Losing a spouse to cancer is an odyssey through the stormiest seas of existence, an experience that can leave you feeling like a ship adrift, tossed by waves of sorrow and uncertainty. Yet, even amidst the tempest, there lies an opportunity for profound self-discovery and growth. In this subchapter, we shall embark on a voyage into the heart of self-awareness and the mastery of our emotions, the very bedrock upon which we shall construct our resilience and foster a positive mindset after the loss of a spouse.

Self-awareness is the lighthouse that guides our ship through the darkness of personal development. It involves plumbing the depths of our thoughts, emotions, and behaviors, and gazing into the mirror of our strengths and weaknesses. As we traverse this inward journey, we uncover the keys to understanding our reactions and patterns, allowing us to make choices consciously aligned with our values and aspirations.

The initial step in our quest to enhance self-awareness is to dedicate time to ponder our emotions and thoughts. Whether through the art of journaling, the serenity of meditation, or the guidance of a therapist or support group, we embark on a sacred pilgrimage into the realm of our feelings. By exploring these emotions and acknowledging the pain that courses through us, we lay the foundation for the gradual mending of our hearts.

Self-regulation, the art of steering our emotional vessel with finesse, is another compass on our journey. After the loss of a spouse, the emotional tempest often engulfs us in a maelstrom of feelings – anger, sadness, and loneliness. It is essential to channel these emotions through healthy outlets, be it the soothing balm of physical activity, the mindfulness that calms the tumultuous sea of our minds, or the guiding hand of professionals when needed.

The tapestry of emotional intelligence weaves through this narrative, a golden thread that binds self-awareness and self-regulation. It is the skill of recognizing and understanding not only our own emotions but also the emotions of others. With emotional intelligence, we navigate the labyrinth of grief more effectively, communicating our needs and boundaries, and building bridges of understanding and connection with those who walk alongside us.

To construct a vessel of resilience that shall withstand the tempestuous sea of loss, we must turn our focus towards the tools of positive mindset and self-belief. These tools allow us to forge our sails from the fabric of challenge, to reframe our perspectives into the guiding stars of hope, and to hoist the banner of our strengths and accomplishments. With this positive mindset, we uncover the treasures of meaning and purpose even amidst the shadows of loss.

In closing, the path towards resilience and a positive mindset after losing a spouse to cancer necessitates the exploration of self-awareness and the mastery of our emotional tides. Through reflection on our emotions, their skillful navigation, and the cultivation of an optimistic outlook, we gradually reconstruct our lives with newfound vigor and purpose. Healing takes time, and the wisdom of seeking support from both loved ones and professionals is a beacon of guidance along the way. With self-awareness as our North Star, we navigate the labyrinth of grief, emerging from the darkness stronger, more resilient, and ready to embrace life anew.

The Art of Weaving a Tapestry of Connection

Losing a cherished one to cancer is akin to navigating the labyrinth of life's most turbulent seas. The gales of pain, the tidal waves of grief, and the overwhelming sense of isolation can cast us adrift, leaving us feeling marooned on an emotional island. However, in the vast ocean of human experience, we are never truly alone. It is the bridges we build, the connections we foster, that become the stars that guide us through the darkest of nights.

In times when we may feel estranged from the world, reaching out to kindred souls who have also tasted the bitterness of loss can be a beacon of light. Joining hands with support groups or seeking solace in online communities dedicated to those who grieve can create a web of empathy and understanding. In the exchange of stories, in listening to the pain of others, and in the act of offering support, we mend our fractured hearts and find strength in shared vulnerability.

Yet, our connections should not be limited to fellow widows and widowers alone. The tapestry of relationships with family, friends, and loved ones who remain by our side is equally vital. These connections are the bedrock upon which we construct the fortress of our healing. They can serve as pillars of support, as long as we are willing to communicate our needs and emotions openly. Like lighthouses, our loved ones can guide us through treacherous waters, but they need our signals to shine their light effectively.

While the hands of others are instrumental in our journey, our own hands must be firm and steady. Losing a spouse can shake our self-confidence and challenge our belief in our ability to navigate life alone. It is in the craft of personal development that we find the tools to rebuild our self-esteem. The art of journaling, the serenity of meditation, or the guidance of professionals form the chisels and brushes with which we sculpt our resilience. Through these practices, we master our emotions, unlock self-awareness, and paint a positive mindset on the canvas of our healing.

Amidst these intricate relationships, the brush of emotional intelligence is our greatest tool. It enables us to communicate our needs effectively, to empathize with others, and to weave the threads of meaningful connections. The canvas of emotional intelligence is painted with the hues of self-reflection, the skill of active listening, and the art of seeking to understand the hearts of others.

In conclusion, the tapestry of our connections is an essential element of the voyage through grief after losing a spouse to cancer. Whether in the embrace of kindred spirits, the bonds of loved ones, or the brushstrokes of personal development, emotional intelligence, and a positive mindset, our journey becomes a collective endeavor. In each other's company, we are not alone; together, we find the strength to weather the storm and bask in the warmth of shared hope.

Practical Alchemy for Healing: Navigating the Abyss of Grief

We embark on a sacred quest to discover the hidden gems of practical alchemy. Here, we will delve into the mystical realm of creative coping strategies that resonate with the magic within each of us. Each of the exercises and tips outlined below are the alchemical tools you have at your disposal, ready to assist you on your transformative journey. Just as an ancient alchemist had a diverse set of tools to transmute base metals into gold, you have a unique set of practices to transmute your grief into resilience. These tools are your companions on the path to healing, ready to be wielded with intention and grace. Let us be like the ancient alchemists, transforming the leaden weight of grief into the golden light of resilience.

Section 1: *The Art of Expressive Alchemy*

Exercise 1: "The Elixir of Expression - The Alchemical Canvas of Healing"

In this enchanting exercise, we delve into the profound art of expressive alchemy. It's as if you stand before the sacred canvas of the universe, a blank page in the book of your soul, yearning to hold the vivid colors of your emotions. Let the brush in your hand be the wand of transformation, and let each stroke be a whisper from the depths of your being.

Step 1: The Canvas of Emotions Imagine a canvas before you, a vast expanse of white, a silent witness to your inner world. As you prepare to paint, remember that this canvas holds the capacity to soak up your emotions, to be the chalice for your pain and, eventually, the crucible for your resilience.

Step 2: The Palette of Transformation Consider the colors you will use. If sorrow has taken root in your heart, let deep blues and purples flow from your brush. These are the colors of the night, of the soul's deep well of emotions. They represent the darkness that has been your companion through the grief.

Step 3: The Alchemical Brushstrokes With each stroke, envision your feelings flowing onto the canvas. As you paint, do not be constrained by the forms or shapes; this is your sacred alchemical work. Your brush is your wand, your emotions are the magic, and the canvas is the stage.

Step 4: The Metaphor of Overpainting Now, here comes the alchemical transformation. When you feel that you've expressed your sorrow fully, it's time to paint over those dark colors. Choose bright yellows and oranges; they symbolize the alchemical process of transmutation, turning lead into gold. These are the colors of healing and resilience.

Step 5: Witness the Alchemy Unfold Step back and observe as your canvas undergoes its alchemical transformation. The deep blues and purples, once heavy with sorrow, are now the rich foundation upon which the golden hues of resilience can shine. This is the alchemical marriage of opposites, the union of your pain and your healing.

Step 6: The Canvas of Healing As you gaze upon your canvas, you are gazing into the mirror of your own soul. The transformation you have created is not just a painting; it is a reflection of your inner journey. You have turned your grief into a masterpiece of resilience. This canvas is not only a work of art but a testament to your alchemical power.

In the grand tapestry of "Eternal Echoes," this exercise serves as a profound reminder that, just like the alchemists of old, you have the power to transmute the leaden weight of grief into the golden light of resilience. Your canvas is but one chapter in the book of your soul, and through the art of expressive alchemy, you continue to write your story of healing, growth, and transformation.

Section 2: The Energetic Alchemy of Healing

Exercise 2: "The Elixir of Self-Care- A Journey of Self-Mastery"

In this section, we journey into the realm of energetic alchemy, where the power of self-healing lies within your grasp. Picture a world where you are both the alchemist and the Master of your own healing journey, and the elixir you brew is one of profound transformation.

Step 1: The Sacred Space: Prepare a tranquil, sacred space where you can embark on your self-Reiki journey. Light candles, burn incense, or simply sit in a space that resonates with peace and serenity. This is your alchemical laboratory, and you are the alchemist in charge.

Step 2: The Healing Intention Set a clear intention for your self-healing session. You are here to transform grief into resilience. Envision your hands as vessels of transformation, akin to the alchemist's flasks. They are the conduits through which life force energy flows, carrying the elixir of healing.

Step 3: Channeling Life Force Energy As you begin your self-Reiki practice, feel the energy within you awakening. Visualize this energy as a river of radiant light, a universal life force, flowing through your hands. In your mind's eye, see it like liquid gold, the alchemical substance of healing.

Step 4: Targeting the Areas of Grief Identify the areas within your body and spirit where grief resides. These are the places that need the alchemical touch of transformation. Place your hands gently on these areas, letting the river of healing light pour into them.

Step 5: Dissipating the Pain As you apply Reiki, imagine the life force energy breaking apart the dense energy of grief. Like a skilled alchemist, watch as the alchemical reaction unfolds. The pain dissipates, turning into vapor, rising and merging with the universal energy.

Step 6: The Elixir of Resilience In the place where grief once resided, there is now a space filled with the elixir of resilience. Visualize it as a radiant, golden light that permeates your entire being. This elixir is the essence of your transformation, a testament to your mastery over the alchemical process.

Step 7: The Self-Care Alchemist As you complete your self-Reiki session, you are not only the alchemist but the elixir itself. You have catalyzed your own healing journey, turning sorrow into strength. In the mirror of your spirit, you see the reflection of the Reiki alchemist, the self-care master.

In "Eternal Echoes," this exercise serves as a reminder that the path of energetic alchemy is one of self-empowerment. Just as the ancient alchemists transmuted base metals into gold, you have the power to transmute your grief into resilience. You are the alchemist of your own story, creating a masterpiece of healing and self-mastery.

Section 3: The Meditation Alchemy of Inner Peace

Exercise 3: "The Alchemical Voyage Within - Communion with the Cosmos"

In this enchanting exercise, we transcend the boundaries of our physical existence and embark on an alchemical journey into the heart of the universe. Picture yourself as a pilgrim, a traveler of the cosmos, on a quest to transmute your grief into resilience through the wonders of nature.

Step 1: Preparation for the Cosmic Sojourn Before you embark on this alchemical voyage, prepare yourself as a humble seeker of the universe's wisdom. Dress comfortably, as you would for any sacred pilgrimage. Leave behind the trappings of your daily life and allow yourself to be fully present in the moment.

Step 2: The Pilgrim's Mindset As you step onto the path of your nature walk, imagine yourself as a pilgrim. Each step is a dance with the divine, and every inhalation of the earth's fragrant air is a sip of celestial elixir. You are not just a wanderer in the woods; you are a cosmic traveler, on a quest to uncover the mysteries of the universe.

Step 3: The Alchemical Whispers of Nature Listen carefully to the rustling leaves, the song of the birds, and the whisper of the wind through the trees. These are not mere sounds; they are the alchemical whispers of the cosmos, guiding you on your transformative journey. Nature is your alchemical laboratory, and it is teeming with secrets waiting to be uncovered.

Step 4: Releasing Your Sorrows to the Earth With each step, feel the weight of your grief and sorrow lifting from your shoulders. Release it to the earth, as if offering it to Mother Nature herself. Imagine the soil absorbing your pain, and the roots of the trees drawing it deep into the earth, where it can be transmuted and transformed.

Step 5: Communion with Mother Nature As you walk, pause to touch the trees, feel the earth beneath your feet, and observe the life that surrounds you. In these moments, you are in communion with Mother Nature, the great alchemist of the natural world. Let her loving arms embrace your pain and sorrow, offering solace and healing.

Step 6: Discovering the Hidden Light In the midst of your nature walk, you may begin to sense a profound shift within you. It's as if the weight of grief has been replaced by a sense of lightness. You are discovering the hidden light within, much like the ancient alchemists turning base metals into gold.

In "Eternal Echoes," this exercise serves as a poignant reminder that the cosmos itself is our partner in the alchemical process of transformation. Nature, the ultimate alchemist, is ever ready to receive our pain and transmute it into healing energy. Through the tapestry of art, energy, intuition, and nature, we become the alchemists of our own lives, crafting the elixir of resilience. As we embrace the alchemy of grief, we unearth the hidden light within, and it becomes our guiding star through the echoes of eternity.

Exercise 4: "The Written Release - Letters to the Beloved Beyond"

In this exercise, we harness the power of words to embark on an intimate journey of healing and connection. As a writer, your pen is your guide through the labyrinth of emotions. Imagine the pages of your journal as a bridge to the world beyond, a place where you can have an ongoing dialogue with your departed loved one.

Step 1: The Sacred Journal Select a journal that resonates with you on a deep level. It is not merely a notebook; it is a vessel for your emotions, a sacred space where you can pour out your heart and soul.

Step 2: The Dialogue of Words Sit in a quiet space where you can fully immerse yourself in the act of writing. Let your pen glide across the pages as if it's a vessel of your deepest thoughts and emotions. Begin by addressing your departed loved one. Use their name or a term of endearment that connects you.

Step 3: Sharing Your Innermost Thoughts With every stroke of the pen, share your innermost thoughts, your joys, your regrets, your gratitude, and your longing. Write about the moments you cherish, the experiences you wish you could have shared, and the wisdom you have gained through your journey of grief.

Step 4: Finding Solace in the Words As you write, you may begin to feel a sense of connection with your departed loved one. It's as if they are listening, their presence filling the room. This written dialogue serves as a powerful way to express your emotions and find solace in the process.

Step 5: Unburdening the Heart Let the pages of your journal become a vessel for your grief. By putting your emotions into words, you unburden your heart, making space for the light of healing to enter. This process can be both a release and a means of connection, a way to keep the memory of your loved one alive.

Step 6: The Ongoing Conversation Remember that this written dialogue can be ongoing. Your journal becomes a cherished companion, a place where you can return whenever you need to connect with your departed loved one. It's a conversation that transcends time and space.

In "Eternal Echoes," this exercise is a testament to the healing power of words and the enduring nature of love. It's a reminder that even in grief, we can find connection and solace through the written word. Just as the ancient scribes preserved the wisdom of the ages, you are preserving the memory and love you shared with your departed loved one, creating a living testimony to the power of the human spirit and the enduring nature of love.

Exercise 5: "Setting Intentions - The Alchemical Alcove of Affirmations"

In this transformative exercise, we tap into the profound power of intention-setting, akin to the ancient alchemists who declared their purpose and set out to transmute the ordinary into the extraordinary. As you embark on this journey of self-discovery and healing, your intentions are the alchemical blueprint, the guiding stars in the night sky of your grief.

Step 1: The Sacred Space of Reflection Find a tranquil and sacred space where you can be fully present in the moment. It's a space where your intentions can take root and flourish, much like the alchemist's laboratory where magical transformations occur.

Step 2: The Alchemical Affirmations Close your eyes and take a few deep breaths. Let go of the external world and turn your gaze inward. With the profound wisdom of your intuition, begin to craft your affirmations. These are not mere words; they are the alchemical spells that will shape your healing journey.

Step 3: The Power of Positivity Frame your intentions in the positive. Instead of stating what you want to release, declare what you want to embrace. For example, rather than saying, "I want to let go of grief," affirm, "I embrace healing and resilience."

Step 4: The Alchemical Precision Be clear and specific in your intentions. Consider the aspects of your healing journey that are most important to you. Let your intuition be your guide. For example, if you wish to find inner peace, affirm, "I am a vessel of inner peace and serenity."

Step 5: The Soul's Resonance As you create your affirmations, ensure that they resonate with your unique path and your emotions. These affirmations are not generic; they are the alchemical keys that unlock your potential for transformation.

Step 6: The Daily Ritual Make your intention-setting a daily ritual, just as the alchemists repeated their processes to refine their work. Recite your affirmations each day, imbuing them with the energy of your spirit and the power of your intention.

In "Eternal Echoes," this exercise is a testament to the fact that we are the alchemists of our own lives. Through intention-setting, you are declaring your purpose and guiding the cosmic energies to transform your grief into resilience. Much like the ancient alchemists who sought to transmute the ordinary into the extraordinary, you are embarking on a journey of self-transformation, where the alchemical power of your intentions is your guiding light through the echoes of eternity.

Exercise 6: "Nature Walk Meditation - The Symphony of Oneness"

In this profound exercise, we invite you to embrace the healing energy of nature as your silent companion. Picture yourself as a wanderer in the cathedral of the natural world, where the rustling leaves, the melodious bird songs, and the gentle whispers of the wind are the sacred hymns of the universe.

Step 1: Choosing Your Sanctuary Select a nearby park or a natural setting that calls to you. It's not just a place; it's a sanctuary for your soul, where you can partake in the divine symphony of nature.

Step 2: The Pilgrim's Stance As you begin your nature walk, adopt the mindset of a pilgrim, a traveler on a sacred journey. Each step is a testament to your reverence for the earth, and every inhalation of the crisp, natural air is a sip of the universe's elixir.

Step 3: Sensory Awakening Allow your senses to awaken to the world around you. As you walk, open your eyes to the sights of the natural world. Notice the vibrant colors, the play of light and shadow, and the intricate details of each leaf and flower.

Step 4: The Symphony of Sounds Listen attentively to the symphony of nature. The birds, the insects, the gentle rustle of leaves in the breeze - they are not mere sounds; they are the notes in the universal melody. Let these sounds wash over you, soothing your spirit.

Step 5: A Touch of Reverence Reach out and touch the earth, the trees, the plants. In these moments, you are in communion with the divine alchemy of nature. Feel the textures, the warmth, the life that surrounds you.

Step 6: Releasing the Weight With each step, release your pain and sorrow to the earth, as if you are offering your burdens to Mother Nature herself. Imagine the soil absorbing your pain, and the roots of the trees drawing it deep into the earth, where it can be transmuted.

Step 7: Oneness with the Universe As you continue your nature walk, you may begin to feel a profound sense of oneness with the universe. It's as if you are no longer a separate entity but a part of the grand tapestry of creation.

In the world of "Eternal Echoes," this exercise is a reminder that in nature, you can find solace, healing, and a sense of oneness with the universe. Nature is the ultimate alchemist, forever transmuting our sorrows into moments of peace and connection. In the symphony of the natural world, you discover that, like the ancient alchemists who sought to transmute base metals into gold, you have the power to transmute your grief into a deeper understanding of the interconnectedness of all things.

Exercise 7: "The Loving-Kindness Meditation - The Alchemical Elixir of Compassion"

In this meditative practice, we venture into the alchemical realm of the heart, where the power of compassion is the elixir that transmutes grief into inner peace and empathy. Picture yourself as a loving alchemist, concocting a transformative potion of well-wishes for yourself and all beings.

Step 1: The Sacred Meditation Space Create a quiet and sacred space where you can fully immerse yourself in this meditation. It's a place where the heart's intentions can be woven into the fabric of the universe.

Step 2: The Compassionate Affirmations Close your eyes and allow your heart to open wide. As you begin your meditation, repeat a series of compassionate affirmations. These words are not just sounds; they are the alchemical spells that will transform your grief into empathy and inner peace.

Step 3: Self-Compassion Begin by directing loving-kindness towards yourself. Offer well-wishes for your own healing and well-being. Repeat affirmations like, "May I be free from suffering. May I find peace and happiness. May I be filled with love and compassion."

Step 4: Expanding Compassion As your heart becomes a wellspring of compassion, extend your well-wishes to others. Start with loved ones, and then gradually expand to acquaintances, strangers, and even those with whom you've had difficulties. The alchemical magic is in your willingness to send loving-kindness to all beings.

Step 5: Transmutation of Grief As you meditate, imagine your grief being transmuted into a warm, golden light of compassion. See it dissipate and transform, much like the alchemist turning base elements into something precious.

Step 6: The Elixir of Inner Peace As you conclude your loving-kindness meditation, you will find that your grief has been replaced by an elixir of inner peace and empathy. This elixir is the testament to your compassionate alchemy, a reminder that you have the power to transform your own suffering into a source of profound empathy and peace.

In "Eternal Echoes," this exercise serves as a poignant reminder that the power of compassion is one of the most profound alchemical tools at your disposal. Just as the ancient alchemists transmuted the ordinary into the extraordinary, you are transmuting your grief into a deeper understanding of the interconnectedness of all beings. Through the practice of loving-kindness, you create a living testament to the power of the human heart and its capacity for transformation and compassion.

Remember that healing is a unique journey, and there's no set timeline. Be patient and gentle with yourself. The power of resilience resides within your ability to embrace the tools and talents that are uniquely yours, allowing them to guide you toward a place of healing and transformation.

Through art, energy healing, intuitive coaching, and a deep connection to the universe, you have the means to navigate your grief and emerge stronger on the other side. The universe has a way of guiding us through the darkest of nights to a new dawn of hope and healing.

CHAPTER 4

Finding Light Amidst Darkness

Amidst the darkest hours of despair, in a relentless quest that led us to explore every possible avenue, we stumbled upon a brilliant doctor—a true beacon of hope. This remarkable physician was a specialist in precision radiotherapy, and she held a conviction that defied all odds. With unwavering determination, she set out to release my husband from the shackles of an inoperable brain tumor, all without the need for any invasive surgery.

It was a daunting endeavor, one we willingly embraced, as we clung to the slender thread of possibility it offered. Over the course of ten arduous office visits for radiotherapy in a hospital setting, we embarked on a journey, each appointment akin to a step towards liberation. In those moments, we became the alchemists of our own narrative. With unwavering faith in the doctor's expertise and the resilience of the human spirit, we began the profound work of transmuting despair into a radiant, unwavering hope. My husband was a real trooper, even though the radiotherapy treatment made him sick to his stomach, he never complained once and always carried with him a beautiful smile.

The unfolding of those ten visits was nothing short of miraculous, a testament to the indomitable power that resides within each of us. It was a story that proved, beyond a shadow of a doubt, that the human spirit can overcome the most formidable challenges, emerging from the crucible of adversity, not weakened, but strengthened and renewed.

Embarking on the Spiritual Odyssey

Picture yourself standing on the precipice of an expansive sea, the weight of grief pressing on your heart. The spiritual odyssey begins at the shores of your soul, where the call for something greater invites you to embark on a profound journey. In these early steps, the exploration of spirituality is not an escape from sorrow but a conscious choice to navigate the depths of the inner seas.

Example - The Sanctuary of Faith:

Meet Mary, a widow navigating the labyrinth of grief. For her, faith became more than a set of doctrines; it transformed into a sanctuary of solace. In the hushed moments of solitude, Mary found herself engaged in a deeply personal dialogue with the divine. Her belief system, rooted in teachings of love and resilience, served as a guiding compass through the tumult. The act of prayer was not a plea to undo grief but a means to find a spiritual anchor within it.

The Alchemy of Belief Systems

Just as the ancient alchemists sought to transmute base metals into gold, those grappling with loss engage in a similar alchemy with their belief systems. Whether through prayer, meditation, or sacred rituals, individuals transmute the raw emotions of grief into a wellspring of spiritual strength. It is not a simplistic process; it is an intricate dance where turning to one's faith becomes a transformative act, mirroring the alchemists' pursuit of turning the ordinary into the extraordinary.

> *Example - A Tapestry of Beliefs:*
>
> Consider David, a widower with a rich tapestry of diverse beliefs. In his journey of healing, he found solace in weaving a narrative that celebrated the common threads of compassion, love, and interconnectedness across different spiritual traditions. His approach became a testament to the inclusive nature of spirituality, showcasing how diverse beliefs could harmoniously coexist in the mosaic of his healing journey.

Faith as a Lighthouse in the Dark

In the tempestuous sea of grief, spirituality serves as the lighthouse piercing through the darkness. It doesn't offer facile answers; instead, it provides a sacred space for introspection, reflection, and communion with something greater than oneself. This facet of the healing journey isn't about escaping grief; it's about finding moments of peace amid the storm.

> *Example - The Garden of Reflection:*
>
> Meet Sarah, mourning the loss of her husband. She created a metaphorical garden of reflection as her sacred space. Within its confines, she engaged in practices like meditation and immersed herself in spiritual texts. This garden wasn't an attempt to evade grief; rather, it served as a sanctuary where she could commune with the divine, finding moments of peace and reflection amid the tumultuous waves of sorrow.

Closing Thoughts: Embracing the Spiritual Alchemy

In the intricate tapestry of healing after losing a spouse to cancer, the role of spirituality, faith, and belief systems is a deeply personal thread. It's not a uniform or prescriptive approach but rather a mosaic of diverse practices, each contributing to the alchemical transformation of grief into a resilient, spiritually enriched existence. As we delve deeper into this dimension of the healing journey, we discover that, much like the ancient alchemists, we possess the power to turn the leaden weight of loss into the golden light of spiritual renewal.

Unveiling the Tapestry of Meaning: A Journey of Rediscovery After Loss

In the wake of profound loss, the search for meaning and purpose becomes a beacon guiding us through the labyrinth of grief. It's a transformative journey that doesn't erase the pain but paints it with hues of significance, allowing us to rediscover the essence of life amid the shadows.

Embarking on the Quest for Meaning

Imagine standing at the crossroads of despair, grappling with the weight of loss. The quest for meaning begins as a courageous journey into the heart of our existence. It's not about escaping sorrow but about navigating through it, seeking the hidden gems of purpose that shimmer in the recesses of our souls.

> *Example - The Phoenix of Purpose:*
>
> Meet Emma, a woman who, after losing her partner, embarked on a quest to find meaning. Instead of succumbing to the ashes of grief, she envisioned herself as a phoenix rising. Emma channeled her pain into a purposeful mission of supporting others through similar struggles. In helping them, she discovered that the ashes of her own sorrow had become the fertile ground for a garden of new beginnings.

Transformative Power of Purpose

In the alchemy of grief, finding purpose is the elixir that transmutes the leaden weight of loss into a golden opportunity for growth. It's a process that doesn't negate the pain but elevates it into a force for positive change. The power lies in recognizing that even the most profound sorrow can be a catalyst for transformative purpose.

> *Example - The Artisan of Adversity:*
>
> Consider Mark, a widower who, in the crucible of his grief, discovered a latent talent for art. His purpose

> became clear as he transformed the canvas of his sorrow into a masterpiece of resilience and beauty. Through his art, Mark not only found solace but also became an inspiration to others navigating the challenging landscapes of loss.

Reveling in the Symphony of Meaning

Finding meaning after loss is akin to composing a symphony where each note of pain contributes to the melody of purpose. It's about understanding that even in the silence between the notes, there lies a profound significance that shapes the composition of our lives.

> *Example - The Musician of Memory:*
>
> Imagine Rachel, who lost her sister to illness. In her grief, she found solace in music. Rachel composed a symphony that encapsulated the memories and emotions she shared with her sister. Each note became a brushstroke on the canvas of her healing, turning the pain of loss into a poignant melody of remembrance.

Closing Crescendo: Inspiring Through Purpose

In the tapestry of life after loss, the power of finding meaning, and purpose is not a mere antidote to grief but a profound revelation of resilience. It's an invitation to become the architects of our destiny, weaving purpose into the very fabric of our existence. As we delve into this transformative journey, we unveil the extraordinary truth that, in the aftermath of loss, we have the capacity to discover new meanings, shape new purposes, and inspire others to embark on their own quests of rediscovery.

Embarking on the Journey within: The Significance of Self-Discovery and Growth After Losing a Loved One to Cancer

In the aftermath of losing a loved one to cancer, the path of self-discovery and personal growth unfolds as a sacred odyssey, a transformative expedition into the depths of one's own being. It's not merely a reaction to grief but a proactive and empowering choice to sculpt a new narrative, to illuminate the shadows with the radiant light of personal evolution.

The Crucial Role of Self-Discovery

Picture standing at the threshold of an undiscovered realm within yourself, the echoes of loss resonating in the corridors of your soul. The importance of self-discovery becomes a guiding star in navigating this uncharted territory. It's an intentional quest to understand, accept, and embrace the evolving self that emerges in the wake of profound loss.

> *Example - The Phoenix of Self-Discovery:*
>
> Meet Alex, a spouse who, after losing their partner to cancer, chose the path of self-discovery. Instead of succumbing to the abyss of grief, Alex envisioned themselves as

> a phoenix rising from the ashes. Through introspection, Alex unearthed passions long dormant, embarked on new adventures, and found solace in self-awareness. The journey within became a testament to the extraordinary resilience that lies dormant within every grieving heart.

The Illuminating Dance of Personal Growth

In the alchemy of grief, personal growth is the luminous metamorphosis that arises from the crucible of pain. It's an intentional and dynamic process that involves not just surviving but thriving in the aftermath of loss. Personal growth becomes the bridge that connects the past with the potential of the future.

> *Example - The Artisan of Adversity:*
>
> Consider Sarah, who, after the loss of her mother to cancer, embraced personal growth as a transformative endeavor. Sarah dedicated herself to learning new skills, exploring uncharted territories of knowledge, and cultivating resilience. Her journey became a testament to the idea that personal growth can be the exquisite artwork crafted from the raw materials of adversity.

The Canvas of Self-Reflection

Self-discovery and personal growth are intricately woven into the fabric of self-reflection. It's about gazing into the mirror of one's own soul, acknowledging the scars of grief, and allowing them to be the brushstrokes that paint a richer and more resilient self-portrait.

> *Example - The Mirror of Healing:*
>
> Imagine David, a son who lost his father to cancer, utilizing self-reflection as a powerful tool for personal growth. David delved into the depths of his emotions, confronted his vulnerabilities, and transformed pain into purpose. His journey of self-discovery became a mirror reflecting not just the scars of loss but the strength that emerged from embracing and navigating those scars.

Closing Symphony: The Enlightening Notes of Transformation

In the tapestry of life after loss, the importance of self-discovery and personal growth is not a mere response to adversity; it's a symphony of enlightenment that inspires the soul to ascend to new heights. It's an invitation to dance with the evolving self, to explore the uncharted territories within, and to embrace the transformation that arises from the alchemy of grief. As we traverse this sacred journey, we discover that within the echoes of loss, there exists a profound harmony, a melody of resilience and self-discovery that inspires and enlightens the spirit.

CHAPTER 5

Building a Supportive Network

Harmony in Grief: The Vital Role of a Support Symphony

In the symphony of grief, the presence of a support system is not merely a comforting melody but a transformative composition that sustains the heart through the profound echoes of loss. It is the intertwining of compassion, understanding, and shared humanity that forms a symphony, echoing the importance of a harmonious support system during the darkest hours.

The Power of Compassionate Companionship:

Imagine grief as a solitary journey through an expansive landscape of sorrow. The significance of a support system becomes the gentle breeze that whispers, "You are not alone." It is compassionate companionship that weaves a comforting melody around the grieving soul, offering solace in the face of the overwhelming silence.

Example - The Winged Shadows of Friendship:

Meet Emily, who lost her brother to a prolonged illness. In the midst of her grief, friends became the winged shadows that lifted her spirit. They didn't shy away from the difficult conversations or uncomfortable silences; instead, they embraced her pain, allowing Emily to navigate the complex landscape of grief with the reassurance that she was supported, understood, and not alone.

The Pillars of Understanding:

In the labyrinth of grief, understanding becomes the sturdy pillars that support the weight of sorrow. A support system that comprehends the nuances of grief provides a stable foundation, preventing the grieving heart from collapsing under the immense burden.

Example - The Fortress of Family:

Consider James, who lost his spouse to cancer. His family became the fortress of understanding, creating a space where James could express his grief without judgment. Their unwavering support formed a fortress that shielded him from the storms of sorrow, allowing James to process and navigate his emotions with the reassurance that his feelings were valid.

Shared Humanity in the Healing Ensemble:

A support system is not just about providing solace; it's about recognizing the shared humanity that connects us all. It is the ensemble of hearts beating in unison, creating a healing melody that resonates with empathy and compassion.

> *Example - The Healing Choir of Community:*
>
> Picture Sarah, a mother who lost her child. The community rallied around her, forming a healing choir that sang songs of empathy and compassion. Through shared experiences, shared tears, and shared moments of silence, the community became an integral part of Sarah's healing journey, reminding her that her grief was acknowledged, and she was surrounded by a chorus of support.

Closing Crescendo: The Resonance of Support:

In the symphony of life after loss, the significance of a support system is not a background hum but a resonant crescendo that uplifts the grieving soul. It is the orchestration of compassion, understanding, and shared humanity that transforms grief from a solo performance into a harmonious ensemble. As we embrace the melody of support, we discover that even in the darkest notes of grief, there exists a profound harmony—a collective resonance that inspires, uplifts, and carries the grieving heart through the echoes of loss.

Navigating the Tapestry of Shared Grief: A Guide to Connecting with Kindred Souls

In the vast landscape of grief, the importance of connecting with others who have weathered similar storms cannot be overstated. It is a journey of shared understanding, a bridge between hearts that have danced with the echoes of loss. Here's a heartfelt guide to help you traverse the delicate terrain of connecting with kindred souls who share the language of grief.

Seeking Shared Spaces of Understanding:

Imagine grief as a vast, unexplored terrain. To connect with others who share similar loss, seek spaces that resonate with understanding. Join support groups, online forums, or local gatherings where the language of grief is spoken fluently. These shared spaces become the meeting grounds where stories are exchanged, tears are understood, and hearts find solace in collective understanding.

> *Example - The Healing Circle:*
>
> Picture Rachel, a woman grieving the loss of her spouse. She found solace in a local grief support circle where individuals, each with their unique story of loss, gathered to share and support. In this healing circle, Rachel discovered that the language of grief transcended words; it was the unspoken understanding that forged connections and provided a sanctuary for healing.

Approaching with Empathy, Not Solutions:

Connecting with others who have experienced similar loss is not about offering solutions or quick fixes; it's about extending the hand of empathy. When reaching out, approach conversations with an open heart, ready to listen without judgment. Shared grief is a delicate dance, and empathy is the music that guides the steps.

> *Example - The Listening Heart:*
>
> Consider Mark, a man who lost his sibling. When connecting with others who shared a similar loss, he approached conversations with a listening heart. Instead of offering advice, he shared his story and listened to theirs. In this exchange of empathy, Mark found that the shared weight of grief became lighter when carried together.

Creating Safe Spaces for Vulnerability:

Connecting with kindred souls in grief requires the cultivation of safe spaces for vulnerability. Encourage open, honest conversations where tears are welcome, and emotions are expressed without fear of judgment. In these safe spaces, the true essence of shared grief unfolds, fostering connections that transcend the surface.

> *Example - The Garden of Vulnerability:*
>
> Imagine Sarah, a mother navigating the loss of her child. She created a metaphorical garden of vulnerability where individuals who had experienced similar loss could openly share their feelings. In this garden, the petals of pain unfolded, and the fragrance of shared understanding blossomed, creating an atmosphere of safety and support.

Embracing the Uniqueness of Each Journey:

While shared grief connects hearts, it's crucial to recognize and honor the uniqueness of each individual journey. Every story of loss is a distinct melody in the symphony of grief, and connecting with others involves respecting the variations in tempo, tone, and rhythm.

> *Example - The Mosaic of Grief:*
>
> Think of James, a widower navigating his grief. As he connected with others who had lost spouses, he embraced the mosaic of grief, acknowledging that each story was a unique piece in the larger picture. This understanding allowed James to appreciate the diverse ways people navigate loss and find common ground while respecting individual nuances.

Closing Harmony: The Language of Shared Loss:

In the realm of connecting with others who have experienced similar loss, remember that grief is a language that doesn't need words to be understood. It's the silent conversations, the shared nods, and the empathetic glances that create a tapestry of shared understanding. As you traverse the delicate terrain of shared grief, may you find comfort, solace, and strength in the connections that echo the language of loss and the resilience of the human spirit.

Navigating the Tapestry of Shared Grief: A Guide to Connecting with Kindred Souls

In the vast landscape of grief, the importance of connecting with others who have weathered similar storms cannot be overstated. It is a journey of shared understanding, a bridge between hearts that have danced with the echoes of loss.

Here's a heartfelt guide to help you traverse the delicate terrain of connecting with kindred souls who share the language of grief.

Seeking Shared Spaces of Understanding:

Imagine grief as a vast, unexplored terrain. To connect with others who share similar loss, seek spaces that resonate with understanding. Join support groups, online forums, or local gatherings where the language of grief is spoken fluently. These shared spaces become the meeting grounds where stories are exchanged, tears are understood, and hearts find solace in collective understanding.

Example - The Healing Circle:

Picture Rachel, a woman grieving the loss of her spouse. She found solace in a local grief support circle where individuals, each with their unique story of loss, gathered to share and support. In this healing circle, Rachel discovered that the language of grief transcended words; it was the unspoken understanding that forged connections and provided a sanctuary for healing.

Approaching with Empathy, Not Solutions:

Connecting with others who have experienced similar loss is not about offering solutions or quick fixes; it's about extending the hand of empathy. When reaching out, approach conversations with an open heart, ready to listen without judgment. Shared grief is a delicate dance, and empathy is the music that guides the steps.

> *Example - The Listening Heart:*
>
> Consider Mark, a man who lost his sibling. When connecting with others who shared a similar loss, he approached conversations with a listening heart. Instead of offering advice, he shared his story and listened to theirs. In this exchange of empathy, Mark found that the shared weight of grief became lighter when carried together.

Creating Safe Spaces for Vulnerability:

Connecting with kindred souls in grief requires the cultivation of safe spaces for vulnerability. Encourage open, honest conversations where tears are welcome, and emotions are expressed without fear of judgment. In these safe spaces, the true essence of shared grief unfolds, fostering connections that transcend the surface.

> *Example - The Garden of Vulnerability:*
>
> Imagine Sarah, a mother navigating the loss of her child. She created a metaphorical garden of vulnerability where individuals who had experienced similar loss could openly share their feelings. In this garden, the petals of pain unfolded, and the fragrance of shared understanding blossomed, creating an atmosphere of safety and support.

Embracing the Uniqueness of Each Journey:

While shared grief connects hearts, it's crucial to recognize and honor the uniqueness of each individual journey. Every story of loss is a distinct melody in the symphony of grief, and connecting with others involves respecting the variations in tempo, tone, and rhythm.

> *Example - The Mosaic of Grief:*
>
> Think of James, a widower navigating his grief. As he connected with others who had lost spouses, he embraced the mosaic of grief, acknowledging that each story was a unique piece in the larger picture. This understanding allowed James to appreciate the diverse ways people navigate loss and find common ground while respecting individual nuances.

Closing Harmony: The Language of Shared Loss:

In the realm of connecting with others who have experienced similar loss, remember that grief is a language that doesn't need words to be understood. It's the silent conversations, the shared nods, and the empathetic glances that create a tapestry of shared understanding. As you traverse the delicate terrain of shared grief, may you find comfort, solace, and strength in the connections that echo the language of loss and the resilience of the human spirit.

10 Tips on communicating with family and friends about your grief and needs

1. Craft Your Emotional Palette:

In the canvas of grief, your emotions are the vibrant hues that paint the landscape of your inner world. Communicate with your loved ones about the shades you're feeling—whether it's the deep blues of sorrow, the fiery reds of anger, or the soft pastels of moments of peace. By expressing the complexity of your emotional palette, you invite them into the rich tapestry of your grief.

2. Share the Chapters of Your Grief Book:

Your grief is a story unfolding, and each chapter reveals a different facet of your journey. Share these chapters with your family and friends—allow them to turn the pages of your grief book. Whether it's a day of profound sadness or a moment of unexpected joy, let them walk alongside you as co-authors, contributing to the narrative with their understanding and support.

3. Be the Composer of Your Boundaries Symphony:

In the symphony of grief, boundaries are the notes that define the melody of your healing process. Communicate your needs clearly—whether it's time alone, moments of shared company, or specific triggers you'd like to avoid. Be the composer of your own symphony, guiding your loved ones in creating a harmonious environment that supports your healing.

4. Illuminate the Path to Support:

Guide your family and friends along the path of support by illuminating what you need. Whether it's a listening ear, a comforting gesture, or practical assistance, communicate these needs openly. By providing them with a roadmap to support, you empower them to be allies in your healing journey.

5. Speak the Language of Vulnerability:

Vulnerability is the universal language of authentic connection. Share your vulnerabilities with your loved ones, expressing the raw and unfiltered aspects of your grief. In doing so, you invite them into the sacred space where honesty fosters understanding, and compassion becomes the bridge between hearts.

6. Embrace the Uniqueness of Each Listener:

Recognize that each family member or friend is a unique listener with their own way of understanding and supporting. Tailor your communication to resonate with their individual qualities and strengths. Embracing this uniqueness cultivates a supportive environment that honors diversity in response and expression.

7. Celebrate the Rituals of Remembrance:

Grief isn't just about the pain; it's also a celebration of the love and memories that endure. Communicate your desire for rituals of remembrance—whether it's lighting a candle, sharing stories, or creating an annual tradition. By involving your loved ones in these rituals, you create a shared space for honoring the legacy of your lost loved one.

8. Foster Open Dialogues of Understanding:

Initiate open dialogues that foster understanding among your family and friends. Encourage them to ask questions, express their concerns, and share their perspectives. In the realm of grief, understanding is the compass that navigates the terrain of emotions, creating pathways for mutual support.

9. Express Gratitude for Their Presence:

In the midst of grief, expressions of gratitude become healing salves for both you and your loved ones. Communicate your appreciation for their presence, acknowledging the support they provide. By doing so, you not only validate their efforts but also cultivate a reciprocal atmosphere of love and understanding.

10. Paint the Future with Hope:

Your journey through grief is a canvas still being painted, and hope is the brush that adds strokes of resilience and possibility. Communicate your hopes for the future with your family and friends. Share the dreams you aspire to pursue and the positive changes you envision. By painting the future with hope, you inspire them to be co-creators of a narrative that transcends the pain of loss.

Closing Note:

In the symphony of grief, communication is the conductor that orchestrates harmony and understanding. As you engage with your family and friends, may your words be melodies of inspiration, fostering connections that transcend the language of loss and echo the resilient spirit within each of you.

CHAPTER 6

Healing Power of a Positive Mindset

The Healing Power of Positivity: My Personal Journey

Navigating the turbulent seas of grief after losing my husband to cancer was a seismic experience that rattled the very foundations of my existence. The profound sense of loss left me adrift in uncertainty, aching to fathom a life without the unwavering support of my partner who had been my rock. In those shadowed moments, I discovered, on an intimately personal level, the extraordinary potency of positivity—a luminous guide steering me toward a future adorned with newfound purpose and happiness.

Positivity, I unearthed, wasn't an ethereal concept but a dynamic force with the power to reshape our mindset and illuminate our outlook on life. It became the catalyst that enabled me to redirect my focus from dwelling on what I had lost to cherishing the remnants, from being engulfed by pain to embracing the potential for growth. Embracing positivity wasn't merely a choice; it emerged as a vital stride in nurturing a resilient mindset, a wellspring of strength propelling me forward.

The expedition to construct a positive mindset after my spouse's departure commenced with a resolute belief in my own capabilities. It was an acknowledgment, both to the universe and to the depths of my soul, that within me resided an inherent reservoir of strength and resilience capable of surmounting this monumental loss. I grasped the power to script my narrative, to compose a tale enriched with joy and fulfillment. It became an affirmation of my ability to rebuild and rediscover happiness.

On this odyssey, emotional intelligence and self-awareness became my steadfast companions. Recognizing and honoring the entirety of my emotional spectrum became crucial—granting myself the liberty to grieve and heal at my own pace. Equally pivotal was the cultivation of self-awareness—the discernment to identify when negative thoughts and emotions threatened to ensnare me. Practicing emotional intelligence positivity and art of reframing negativity, replacing it with affirmations of positivity, and anchoring my focus on gratitude for the present.

The radiance of positivity, I realized, transcended my individual sphere; it was infectious. Immersing myself in a cocoon of positive influences, be it through the embrace of supportive friends and family or engaging in personal development activities, revealed an abundant source of resilience. Seeking communities and support groups where kindred spirits shared analogous journeys provided empathy and a wellspring of inspiration.

Crucially, recognizing the power of positivity wasn't a call to stifle or overlook my grief. It was, instead, an invitation to acknowledge the pain, to feel its depths, while concurrently choosing to spotlight the expansive horizons of possibilities. By crafting a positive mindset, holding a steadfast belief in myself, and diligently practicing emotional intelligence, I embarked on the arduous yet profoundly rewarding journey of reconstructing my life after bidding farewell to my beloved husband.

Embracing the power of positivity has since become my guiding star—a luminous force stirring the resilience within me, steering me towards a future adorned with love, happiness, and an abiding sense of purpose. This narrative is a testament to the latent strength residing within each of us, waiting to be stirred by the transformative power of positivity.

Exploring the role of mindset in the healing process:

Embark with me on a journey through the labyrinth of healing, where the tapestry of recovery is woven by the intricate threads of mindset. Delve into the very essence of this exploration as we unravel the profound role that mindset plays in the intricate dance of healing after profound loss.

In the alchemy of healing, mindset is not just a fleeting thought or a passing notion; it is the maestro orchestrating the symphony of recovery. The compass guides the ship through the stormy seas of grief, steering it towards calmer waters where healing can unfurl its delicate wings.

Mindset, I have discovered, is the subtle architect shaping the landscape of our emotional terrain. It is the lens through which we perceive the world, a kaleidoscope that can transform the hues of pain into the palette of resilience. How we choose to frame our thoughts, how we cultivate our mental landscape, becomes the brush that paints the masterpiece of our healing journey.

In the realm of mindset, there exists an artistry of perception. It's not about denying the existence of pain or glossing over the challenges; rather, it's a conscious choice to frame our experiences in a way that nurtures growth. It's about looking beyond the shadows of grief and discerning the faint glimmers of hope that dance in the periphery.

The role of mindset, I've come to realize, extends beyond mere positive thinking. It is a profound recognition that our thoughts are not passive spectators but active participants in the process of healing. It's the understanding that, by cultivating a mindset attuned to resilience, we invite the healing energies of the universe to intertwine with our own.

In the crucible of grief, mindset becomes the silent companion, whispering words of encouragement when the night is darkest. It is the anchor that grounds us in the belief that, even in the face of profound loss, there exists a reservoir of strength within. The healing process, therefore, becomes a testament to the transformative power of a mindset sculpted with intention and fortified with unwavering belief.

As we explore the role of mindset in the healing process, let us unravel the threads of resilience, the stitches of hope, and the brushstrokes of a mindset that transforms adversity into a canvas of renewal. This exploration is an invitation to dance with the alchemy of our own thoughts, to embrace the role of mindset as a vital partner in the symphony of healing after the echoes of loss have reverberated through our souls.

Explaining how thoughts and beliefs can influence one's experience of grief.

In the profound tapestry of grief, the threads of thoughts and beliefs weave a narrative that profoundly influences the landscape of our experience. Imagine this intricate tapestry as a canvas where emotions, like vivid pigments, are splashed across the surface. Each stroke, each hue, is not merely a reflection of our external reality but an interplay of our internal thoughts and beliefs, shaping the very essence of our journey through loss.

Consider a thought as a seed planted in the fertile soil of our minds. It can blossom into a vibrant flower or morph into an invasive weed, casting shadows on the emotional terrain. For instance, the thought, "I should have done more," might blossom into a flower of remorse, coloring the canvas with shades of guilt. Conversely, the thought, "I cherish the moments we shared," could bloom into a flower of gratitude, casting a warm glow on the emotional landscape.

Beliefs, on the other hand, are like the overarching branches of a tree, providing structure and shade to the thoughts beneath. If the belief is, "I'll never find happiness again," it casts a heavy shadow, obscuring the potential for joy even in the smallest moments. Conversely, a belief like, "Through healing, I can rediscover happiness," acts as a sturdy bough, allowing the sunlight of hope to filter through.

Now, let's delve into how this interplay unfolds in the realm of grief. Picture a moment of reminiscence, where the tapestry of memories is draped over the canvas of your mind. If the thought that accompanies it is, "I'll never overcome this pain," it casts a somber tone, tainting the memory with a sense of hopelessness. However, if the accompanying thought is, "In honoring their memory, I find strength," it transforms the memory into a beacon of resilience, illuminating the emotional landscape.

Moreover, beliefs can act as lenses through which we view our grief. If the belief is, "Grieving should be a silent, solitary process," it frames the experience with isolation. However, if the belief is, "Through shared experiences, grief becomes a communal journey," it reframes the narrative, fostering connection and support.

Consider this analogy: thoughts and beliefs are the architects of the emotional architecture we inhabit during grief. They construct the rooms of sorrow, hope, guilt, and resilience. For instance, the thought, "I can't bear this pain," might build a room of despair, while the belief, "With time, I can navigate through grief," constructs a room of resilience.

In the symphony of grief, thoughts, and beliefs are the melodies that echo through our hearts. By cultivating awareness of these internal orchestrations, we become the conductors, guiding the emotional symphony toward harmony and healing. Remember, the canvas is ever-evolving, and in the brushstrokes of your thoughts and beliefs, you hold the power to paint a narrative of grief that is not defined solely by loss but also by the resilience and transformation that can emerge from the shadows.

The power to choose our mindset

Now, let us unravel the profound idea that amidst the intricate tapestry of grief, we are not passive spectators but empowered creators, wielding the brush of choice to paint our mindset. In the kaleidoscope of thoughts and beliefs, we hold the palette, and it is within our grasp to choose the hues that will adorn our emotional canvas.

Imagine standing at the crossroads of two divergent paths—one leading to a mindset shrouded in shadows, the other illuminated by the warm glow of resilience. The power to choose beckons us in this pivotal moment. The first path may be paved with thoughts like, "This pain is insurmountable," and beliefs such as, "I am forever bound by grief." It's a path where the emotional landscape remains obscured by the weight of despair.

Now, envision the alternative—the path bathed in the luminosity of choice. Here, thoughts like, "I can find strength in honoring their memory," and beliefs such as, "Through healing, I can shape my narrative," cast a radiant glow on the journey. It's a path where the emotional landscape is infused with the transformative power of resilience and hope.

Consider the analogy of a sculptor carving a masterpiece from a block of marble. Our mindset, like this uncarved block, is a malleable substance waiting to be shaped by the chisel of intention. We have the agency to chip away at the thoughts that do not serve our healing, unveiling the sculpture of a mindset adorned with strength and positivity.

In this journey of choice, the canvas of our grief becomes a mirror reflecting not only the pain of loss but also the resilience of the human spirit. The empowering truth is that we can choose thoughts that foster growth and beliefs that act as pillars of support. It's akin to stepping into the role of an artist who, with each stroke, transforms a blank canvas into a masterpiece of healing.

This idea invites us to embrace the notion that even in the throes of grief, we possess the autonomy to select the emotional palette that will color our experience. The brush of choice is not merely a tool; it is a magical wand that, when wielded with intention, can conjure a mindset capable of navigating the labyrinth of loss with grace and strength.

As we stand before this canvas of choice, let's acknowledge the power within to cultivate a mindset not defined by the circumstances of loss but sculpted by the intentional strokes of resilience and hope. The invitation is extended—to become the architects of our emotional architecture, to wield the brush with purpose, and to choose a mindset that transforms the echoes of grief into a symphony of healing.

The Art of Gratitude: Illuminating the Path to Resilience

Navigating the abyss of grief after the profound loss of my spouse to cancer felt like standing on ground that had crumbled beneath me, leaving me adrift in a sea of shattered emotions. The relentless tide of grief threatened to engulf me, and in those despairing moments, the mere notion of finding hope or positivity seemed as distant as a mirage on the horizon. Yet, it was amidst this profound despair that I uncovered a profound tool on our journey toward healing and resilience – the exquisite art of gratitude and appreciation.

Gratitude, at its core, is the act of acknowledging and treasuring the goodness that still lingers in our lives, no matter how seemingly minuscule. It's about redirecting our gaze from the gaping chasm of loss to the reservoir of abundance that persists. While it may appear counterintuitive to seek gratitude amidst profound loss, it is precisely during these trying times that this practice takes on unparalleled significance.

In actively cultivating gratitude, we embark on a transformative journey to rewire our minds, compelling them to pivot toward the brighter facets of our lives. This isn't about shunning or suppressing our grief; it's about finding a harmonious balance between acknowledging our pain and discovering those moments of solace and joy. It is, fundamentally, a homage to our loved ones—a testament to uncovering meaning and purpose in our own lives.

Practicing gratitude is an art expressed in myriad forms. It can be as straightforward as maintaining a gratitude journal, where each day we inscribe three things for which we are grateful. Our gratitude extends its tendrils through acts of kindness, a lifeline to others navigating the treacherous terrain of grief or a tribute to the causes our late spouse held dear.

Mindfulness and meditation become sacred rituals grounding us in the present moment, unveiling the profound beauty and wonder life continues to bestow.

Crucially, practicing gratitude isn't about negating or denying our pain; it's an expansion of our emotional repertoire—a canvas allowing us to experience moments of joy alongside our grief. It's a profound reminder that even in the darkest nights, stars of goodness and beauty still twinkle in the vast expanse of the world.

Incorporating gratitude and appreciation into our lives after losing a spouse to cancer is a transformative journey. It acts as a catalyst for crafting a positive mindset, nurturing resilience, and fostering self-belief. Moreover, it serves as a beacon enhancing our emotional intelligence and self-awareness, equipping us to navigate the labyrinth of grief with unwavering compassion and profound understanding.

While the path to healing may indeed be long and fraught with challenges, the practice of gratitude and appreciation stands as an unwavering source of strength and resilience, illuminating the way forward. It's a powerful instrument that enables us to honor our loved ones while simultaneously unearthing hope and meaning in our own lives.

Emerging from the Shadows: A Personal Odyssey Towards Fostering Optimism and Hope

The loss of my spouse to cancer shattered the essence of my being, leaving even the most resilient among us feeling as delicate as glass on the brink of breaking. The expedition through grief is as individual as a fingerprint, a labyrinthine tapestry of emotions and experiences. Yet, a singular truth radiates brilliantly through the darkness: cultivating optimism and hope is the key to reconstructing life in the wake of such a soul-wrenching loss. Join me on this transformative odyssey as we explore the resilience that resides within and unveil the path to nurturing a positive mindset, even amidst the most profound shadows.

When grief wraps its heavy cloak around you, it's only natural to be swallowed by a tumult of emotions—sadness, anger, despair—emotions that often seem inescapable, dictating the course of your life. However, it's crucial to remember that these emotions, as all-encompassing as they may be, are not the architects of your future. Through the cultivation of optimism, you can gradually recalibrate your compass toward a brighter horizon. Start by acknowledging the pain, by granting yourself the grace to grieve, while also whispering to your own heart that healing is not just a distant promise; it is a tangible reality waiting to embrace you.

The construction of a positive mindset after the loss of a spouse is a tapestry woven with threads of self-belief and a willingness to take even the smallest steps forward. Envelop yourself in a sanctuary of friends and family who understand, who offer solace, and who encourage your every breath. Engage in activities that once brought you joy, even if their resonance has dimmed in the shadow of your loss. Through these purposeful steps into the light, you'll gradually rewire your very brain, infusing it with the essence of hope and optimism.

Emotional intelligence and self-awareness become the guiding stars in this journey. Take the time to untangle the threads of your emotions and thoughts, and practice self-compassion. It's acceptance that acts as the bridge—acceptance that life has irrevocably changed, but also the recognition that you possess the strength and resilience to adapt, to evolve, to take that first step and many more. By welcoming your emotions without judgment, you gain clarity, a deeper insight into your own personal growth.

In the construction of a positive mindset, negative thoughts stand as formidable adversaries—ones we can challenge and eventually triumph over. Setbacks, we understand, are the natural undulations of life, but they are not destiny's final word. Replace the whispers of self-doubt with the resounding chorus of self-belief. Remind yourself of the strengths, the qualities that have carried you through past tempests. Focus on your inner fortitude, on the feats you've accomplished, and watch as resilience blooms, cradling the tender bud of hope for the future.

In conclusion, even after losing a loved one to cancer, the seeds of optimism and hope can be sown. Through the embrace of personal development, the nurturing of a positive mindset, and the cultivation of emotional intelligence and self-awareness, you can rebuild your life. In the face of life's tempests, never forget that you are a force to be reckoned with, a harbinger of a brighter dawn. Hope, eternal and unwavering, is your constant companion on this sacred journey."

CHAPTER 7

Embracing Healing Modalities

Embarking on the journey of healing after the profound loss of a spouse to cancer is akin to navigating a complex labyrinth of emotions, and in this intricate dance with grief, various healing modalities emerge as beacons of solace and transformation. Let's unfurl the tapestry of these modalities, each a unique brushstroke in the portrait of resilience.

1. Meditation: The Sacred Silence

Picture a serene garden within the realm of your mind, where the gentle rustle of leaves and the distant melody of a babbling brook create a sanctuary for your wounded spirit. Meditation, the art of cultivating inner stillness, becomes the pathway to this sacred space. Whether guided or in silent communion with your own thoughts, meditation allows you to traverse the landscapes of grief with a mindful presence. In the cocoon of quiet introspection, you find moments of respite, clarity, and a gentle unfolding of acceptance.

In the sacred theater of the mind, meditation unfolds as a timeless symphony, orchestrating a harmonious dance between the cacophony of grief and the gentle cadence of inner stillness. Imagine yourself seated in the center of this ethereal auditorium, each breath a note, each heartbeat a melody. Through the art of meditation, you conduct the symphony, allowing the quietude to permeate the raw edges of sorrow. In this serene space, you discover the restorative power of simply being, transcending tumultuous emotions and embracing the melody of acceptance. As you breathe, you become the composer of your own resilience, crafting a serene opus that resonates with the healing vibrations of the universe.

2. Reiki: Channeling the Energy of Healing

Imagine a gentle, yet powerful, current of energy flowing through your being, a cosmic force that seeks to restore balance and harmony. Reiki, a healing modality that channels universal life force energy through the hands, becomes the gentle caress of solace on your journey. As a Reiki Master, envision yourself as both the vessel and the alchemist, allowing this energy to permeate the areas where grief resides. Feel the subtle shifts as the energy dissolves pain and sorrow, replacing them with a radiant well-being. It's a dance with the unseen, a universal embrace that whispers, "You are not alone."

Picture yourself as a weaver, fingers delicately entwining threads of cosmic energy into the fabric of your existence. Reiki becomes the loom through which these threads intertwine, creating a tapestry of healing light. Envision the energy as luminescent strands, each touch of your hands a gentle stroke that unravels the knots of grief. In this dance, you become the artist of your own renewal, the channel through which the universal life force flows. As you immerse yourself in this energetic embrace, feel the alchemy of transformation, the dissipation of darkness, and the emergence of a vibrant, resilient spirit. With each session, you're not merely a recipient but an active participant in the healing process.

3. Therapy: The Art of Verbal Alchemy

Enter the sacred space of a therapist's office, where words become brushstrokes painting the canvas of your healing. Therapy, be it individual or group, provides a platform for the expression of grief in its raw authenticity. The therapist becomes a guide, navigating the labyrinth of emotions with you, unraveling the knots of sorrow, anger, and confusion. Through verbal alchemy, the narrative transforms, and you begin to articulate the unspoken pain, forging a path towards understanding, acceptance, and eventual resilience.

Step into the realm of therapy as a voyager navigating the turbulent seas of the soul. The therapist becomes your guide, equipped not with a compass but with the profound alchemy of words. Picture the therapist as a linguistic alchemist, helping you transmute the leaden weight of grief into the golden understanding of self. As you articulate your pain, each word becomes a beacon illuminating the uncharted territories of your emotions. In this verbal alchemy, the therapist becomes a companion in the excavation of buried feelings, unveiling the gems of insight and resilience. Through the therapeutic dialogue, you embark on a transformative journey, shedding the layers of anguish and emerging as the empowered author of your story.

4. Art Therapy: Expressing the Unspoken

Envision a blank canvas as a mirror reflecting the landscape of your emotions. Art therapy, a form of expression beyond words, becomes the palette through which you can convey the ineffable. Whether through painting, sculpting, or other artistic endeavors, this modality invites you to externalize the internal, giving form to the shapeless contours of grief. The creative process becomes a dialogue with your inner world, a visual narrative of the healing journey. In each stroke and texture, you discover layers of emotions waiting to be acknowledged and transformed.

As you weave these modalities into the fabric of your healing journey, remember that there's no one-size-fits-all approach. Each modality is a unique brush in your artistic palette, allowing you to craft a personalized masterpiece of resilience. Embrace the diversity of these healing modalities, exploring the nuances of meditation, the energy dance of Reiki, the verbal alchemy of therapy, and the expressive canvas of art therapy. Together, they form a symphony of healing, resonating with the rhythm of your journey toward renewed strength and profound transformation.

You enter the studio of art therapy as an artist, not defined by skill but by the authenticity of expression. Imagine your emotions as vibrant pigments waiting to be brushed onto the canvas of healing. In this visual dialogue, you pick up the brushes and sculpt the formless feelings into tangible artworks. As you engage with the creative process, witness the alchemy unfold—the sorrowful strokes giving way to hues of hope, the chaotic splatters transforming into a coherent narrative. Art therapy becomes the sanctuary where your emotions transcend the confines of language, creating a visual testament to your journey. In each creation, you embody the artist of resilience, transforming the intangible into a masterpiece that speaks to the soul.

In these modalities, you are not a passive observer but an active participant, shaping the narrative of your healing journey. Whether orchestrating the symphony of stillness, weaving threads of cosmic connection, engaging in the verbal alchemy of liberation, or painting with the palette of emotions, each modality becomes a brushstroke in the masterpiece of your resilience. Embrace these modalities as partners in your transformative journey, allowing the creative forces within you to unfurl the tapestry of healing, one inspired brushstroke at a time.

Few anecdotes and success stories related to these practices

1. Meditation: The Blossoming Lotus

In the quaint town of Serenity Springs, lived Amelia, a widow navigating the tumultuous waves of grief after losing her husband, Jonathan. Desperate for solace, she discovered the transformative power of meditation. Every morning, under the ancient willow tree by the river, Amelia sat in quiet contemplation. As the days passed, she felt an inner calm blossoming, like a lotus emerging from the mud. Meditation became her sanctuary, and in its embrace, she found the strength to face each day. Amelia's journey inspired others in Serenity Springs, creating a ripple effect of resilience that turned the town into a haven of hope.

2. Reiki: The Healing Hands of Grace

In the bustling city of Radiance Heights, Mark, a grieving widower, sought refuge in the art of Reiki. Through the gentle touch of a Reiki practitioner named Grace, Mark felt a subtle yet profound shift in his energy. With each session, the pain that gripped his heart began to loosen its hold. Inspired by his transformation, Mark decided to become a Reiki practitioner himself. His hands, once heavy with grief, now became conduits of healing for others. Mark's story illuminated the radiant potential within us all, proving that the healing energy of Reiki could not only mend broken spirits but also ignite a chain reaction of compassion and self-discovery.

3. Therapy: The Phoenix's Narrative

In the quaint village of Phoenix Haven, Sarah, a grieving widow, embarked on a therapeutic journey with Dr. Harper, a compassionate psychologist. Through the cathartic process of verbal alchemy, Sarah unraveled the layers of her pain. As she shared her story, a narrative of resilience emerged—a phoenix rising from the ashes of sorrow. Sarah's transformation mended her spirit and inspired the village to view therapy not as a sign of weakness but as a courageous step toward healing. Dr. Harper's office became a sanctuary where stories of rebirth were written, echoing the truth that within the cocoon of vulnerability, one could emerge as a resilient butterfly.

4. Art Therapy: The Canvas of Renewal

In the artistic town of Palette Springs, Alex, a widowed artist, discovered the healing potential of art therapy. Turning the pain of loss into a palette of emotions, Alex expressed the depths of sorrow and the glimmers of hope on canvas. The town embraced Alex's creations, and soon, art therapy workshops flourished. The streets became a gallery of resilience, adorned with the collective artworks of those who had turned their pain into masterpieces. Alex's journey showed that the canvas of renewal isn't just a personal space; it's a communal celebration of strength, where each stroke contributes to the vibrant tapestry of healing.

These anecdotes from various corners of the world exemplify the transformative potential of meditation, Reiki, therapy, and art therapy. Each story is a testament to the resilience that can bloom in the wake of grief, inspiring individuals, and entire communities to embrace these practices as catalysts for healing and renewal.

CHAPTER 8

The Universal Laws of Healing

Unveiling the Divine Symphony: Healing through the 12 Universal Laws

In the tapestry of existence, the 12 Universal Laws resonate as the unseen orchestrators, guiding the dance of galaxies and the ballet of atoms. Yet, within them lies a symphony of healing, an intricate melody that reverberates through the very fabric of our being. Let us embark on a celestial journey, exploring how these laws intricately weave into the narrative of resilience and restoration.

1. The Law of Divine Oneness: The Threads of Connection

Imagine standing beneath the expansive night sky, where each star is not just a distant light but a manifestation of the same cosmic energy that courses through your veins. The Law of Divine Oneness teaches us that all is connected, and in the realm of healing, this law reminds us that our journey is intertwined with the dance of the universe. Through this awareness, we find solace in the shared human experience, a collective heartbeat echoing the rhythm of existence.

> *Example: Sarah, amidst the isolation of her grief, attended a support group where stories of shared pain created a cosmic connection. In the tears of others, she found the reflection of her own sorrow, realizing that, in grief, she was not alone but part of a cosmic chorus.*

2. The Law of Vibration: Harmonizing the Frequencies of Healing

Picture a pond, disturbed by the gentle ripple of a pebble's touch. The Law of Vibration elucidates that everything is in constant motion, emitting its unique frequency. In the healing journey, this law invites us to attune our vibrations to the frequencies of positivity and resilience, creating a harmonic resonance that echoes through the chambers of our soul.

> *Example: Alex, a grief-stricken artist, immersed herself in the act of painting. With each brushstroke, she felt the vibration of colors transforming her sorrow into a symphony of hues. The canvas became a vibrational portrait of her healing journey.*

3. The Law of Correspondence: As Above, So Below

Gaze upon the reflection of a tranquil lake, mirroring the expanse of the sky above. The Law of Correspondence whispers that the patterns of the cosmos are mirrored in the microcosms of our existence. In healing, it guides us to seek harmony within, to the ethereal dance within mirrors.

> *Example: James, guided by the Law of Correspondence, explored the constellations in the night sky and discovered patterns that echoed the ebbs and flows of his emotions. Aligning his inner world with the cosmic rhythm, he found a compass to navigate the seas of grief.*

4. The Law of Attraction: Manifesting Resilience

Envision a garden where the seeds you plant burgeon into vibrant blooms. The Law of Attraction beckons us to recognize the magnetic power of our thoughts and emotions. In healing, it prompts us to cultivate the fertile soil of positivity, attracting the blossoms of resilience and hope.

> *Example: Maria, widowed and seeking solace, embraced the Law of Attraction. Through daily affirmations, she cultivated a mindset that attracted moments of joy. Soon, her life became a garden of resilience, each bloom a testament to the magnetic power of her thoughts.*

5. The Law of Inspired Action: Dancing with the Galactic Flow

Consider a river, flowing effortlessly toward its destination. The Law of Inspired Action urges us to move in harmony with the spiritual current. In healing, it encourages us to take purposeful steps, guided not by haste but by the rhythm of inspired, intentional action.

> *Example: Thomas, grieving the loss of his partner, engaged in acts of kindness inspired by the cosmic flow. Each gesture became a step in the dance of healing, a testament to the transformative power of intentional action.*

6. The Law of Perpetual Transmutation of Energy: Alchemy of Emotions

Picture a phoenix rising from the ashes, embodying the eternal dance of transformation. The Law of Perpetual Transmutation of Energy illuminates the alchemical nature of our emotions. In healing, it teaches us to transmute the lead of sorrow into the gold of resilience, embracing the ever-changing nature of our energetic states.

> *Example: Sophie, touched by the Law of Transmutation, channeled her grief into writing. Through the expressive alchemy of words, she transformed the weight of her emotions into a narrative of resilience, witnessing the transmutation of pain into purpose.*

7. The Law of Cause and Effect: The Echo

Imagine tossing a stone into a pond and witnessing the ripple effect. The Law of Cause and Effect underscores the interconnected dance of actions and consequences. In healing, it calls us to recognize the cosmic echo of our choices, fostering mindfulness in our journey toward resilience.

> *Example: Robert, grieving the loss of his spouse, embraced the Law of Cause and Effect. Consciously choosing compassion and self-care, he witnessed the ripple effect as his actions not only healed himself but also influenced the healing journey of those around him.*

8. The Law of Compensation: Balancing Act

Contemplate the delicate balance of nature, where ecosystems harmonize through give-and-take. The Law of Compensation illuminates the balancing act, reminding us that our efforts toward healing are met with compensation. In resilience, it assures us that the universe acknowledges and reciprocates our strides.

> *Example: Olivia, a widow embracing the Law of Compensation, found solace in supporting others through grief. As she gave, the cosmic balance responded, bringing unexpected moments of comfort and connection into her own life.*

9. The Law of Relativity: The Tapestry of Perspective

Peer through a telescope at distant galaxies, recognizing the vastness of the cosmic tapestry. The Law of Relativity encourages us to view our challenges in the context of the infinite cosmos. In healing, it teaches us that our struggles are relative, inviting us to shift our perspective and find strength in comparison to the grandeur of the cosmic dance.

> *Example: Michael, grappling with loss, invoked the Law of Relativity during a stargazing night. His grief, seen against the backdrop of the universe, transformed into a manageable thread in the cosmic tapestry of existence.*

10. The Law of Polarity: Embracing Dualities

Picture a day seamlessly transitioning into night, an eternal ballet of polarities. The Law of Polarity reveals that opposites coexist, and in the realm of healing, it prompts us to embrace the dualities of joy and sorrow. In resilience, it teaches us that within the darkest nights, the brightest stars of hope flicker.

Example: Emily, guided by the Law of Polarity, found solace in acknowledging the coexistence of joy within grief. Her moments of laughter, though seemingly contrasting, became beacons of light in the profound darkness of her loss.

11. The Law of Rhythm: The Heartbeat

Close your eyes and feel the rhythm of your heartbeat, an everlasting dance of rise and fall. The Law of Rhythm teaches us that life unfolds in rhythmic patterns. In healing, it invites us to recognize the cadence of our journey, understanding that even in the lowest notes, the promise of a harmonious ascent exists.

Example: David, grieving the loss of his spouse, attuned himself to the Law of Rhythm. Through meditation, he synchronized his heartbeat with the cosmic rhythm, finding solace in the understanding that every low note of grief was followed by the promise of a harmonious rise.

12. The Law of Gender: Cosmic Creation

Envision the dance of cosmic energies intertwining in a perpetual embrace. The Law of Gender celebrates the cosmic creation that emerges from the union of masculine and feminine energies. In healing, it reminds us that within the cosmic dance of creation, we are co-creators of our own resilience.

Example: Rachel, a widow embracing the Law of Gender, found empowerment in balancing the energies of action and receptivity. Through this cosmic dance, she became a cocreator of her healing journey, manifesting resilience through the harmonious union of energies.

In the heavenly ballet of healing, the 12 Universal Laws emerge as guiding constellations, illuminating the path toward resilience and restoration. As we navigate the currents of existence, may these laws be our celestial companions, whispering the secrets of the cosmic symphony that heals and transforms. In their dance, we find not only guidance but also the echoes of eternity, resonating with the eternal heartbeat of the universe.

Cosmic Alignment Practices: Bridging the Celestial Laws with Practical Techniques

Embarking on a journey of cosmic alignment involves not only understanding the 12 Universal Laws but also integrating them into our daily lives. These practical exercises serve as celestial keys, unlocking the cosmic potential within each of us.

1. The Law of Divine Oneness: Vast Connection Meditation

Technique: Find a quiet space, close your eyes, and visualize a radiant light connecting you to the cosmos. Inhale, feeling the universal energy entering your being. As you exhale, release any feelings of isolation. With each breath, affirm your connection to the tapestry of existence.

2. The Law of Vibration: Harmonizing Sound Bath

Technique: Engage in sound therapy using singing bowls, chimes, or calming music. Close your eyes, letting the vibrations wash over you. Imagine these vibrations resonating with your emotions, gradually harmonizing your inner frequencies.

3. The Law of Correspondence: Celestial Reflection Journaling

Technique: Reflect on a challenging emotion you're experiencing. Write about how this emotion mirrors a celestial pattern, like the phases of the moon or the changing seasons. Recognize the interconnected symphony between your internal world and the universal order.

4. The Law of Attraction: Magical Vision Board

Technique: Create a vision board that aligns with your healing goals. Include images, words, and symbols representing the positive outcomes you wish to attract. Place it in a visible spot, allowing the universe to manifest these intentions.

5. The Law of Inspired Action: Powerful Mandala Creation

Technique: Design a mandala that symbolizes your journey toward healing. As you draw or paint, infuse each stroke with intentional energy. See the mandala as a map guiding your inspired actions on the path of resilience.

6. The Law of Perpetual Transmutation of Energy: Alchemical Breathwork

Technique: Practice mindful breathing, envisioning each inhale as cosmic energy infusing you with strength. As you exhale, visualize releasing old, stagnant energy associated with grief. Feel the alchemical transformation within with each breath.

7. The Law of Cause and Effect: Celestial Ripple Effect Exercise

Technique: Perform a small act of kindness for someone in your life or a stranger. Acknowledge the positive ripple effect this action creates in the divine order. Witnessing the effects of your kindness reinforces the interconnected dance of cause and effect.

8. The Law of Compensation: Gratitude Ritual

Technique: Before bedtime, express gratitude for three cosmic gifts of the day. Whether it's a supportive friend, a moment of joy, or a newfound insight, recognize the compensation that life offers in response to your healing efforts.

9. The Law of Relativity: Perspective Shift

Technique: When faced with a challenge, consciously shift your perspective by contemplating the vastness of the cosmos. Consider how your current situation fits into the grand scheme, reminding yourself of the relative nature of your experience.

10. The Law of Polarity: Yin-Yang Balance

Technique: Embrace the yin-yang symbol as a representation of balance. In moments of emotional intensity, visualize the dualities. Recognize that even in grief, seeds of joy are waiting to sprout.

11. The Law of Rhythm: Lunar Cycle Reflection

Technique: Observe the phases of the moon, noting its rhythmic cycle. Reflect on your emotional journey in alignment with the lunar phases. Recognize that, like the moon, your healing journey has its own rhythm.

12. The Law of Gender: Celestial Balance Dance

Technique: Engage in a dance or movement practice, embodying the energies of both masculine and feminine. Feel the balance within your movements, recognizing the power of harmonizing these energies for holistic healing.

Integrating these alignment practices into your daily routine transforms the abstract concepts of the 12 Universal Laws into tangible tools for healing. As you engage with these techniques, remember that the universe itself is your co-conspirator in the dance of resilience, offering cosmic guidance and support on your journey.

CHAPTER 9

Honoring the Eternal Echoes

Embracing Eternity: The Everlasting Presence of Our Loved Ones

In the vast tapestry of the universe, where the threads of time and space weave a story beyond our mortal understanding, there exists a realm untouched by the hands of temporal constraints. It's a realm where the essence of our loved ones, those who have traversed the cosmic expanse into the great unknown, finds its eternal abode – in the sanctuary of our hearts and the corridors of cherished memories.

As we navigate the landscape of grief, it becomes a profound revelation that the departure of our loved ones is not a cessation but a transformation. Their physical form may have merged with the cosmic dust, yet the energy, the love, and the laughter that defined them transcends the boundaries, becoming an integral part of the cosmic symphony that plays within us.

Echoes of Love:

Picture an echo, a resonance reverberating through the corridors of time. It's the laughter of a shared moment, the gentle touch of a loving hand, and the warmth of a gaze that spoke volumes without uttering a word. These resonances are not mere memories; they are the very fabric of our existence, interwoven with the stardust of our shared journey.

In the waltz of life and death, our loved ones take on a role akin to celestial guides, orchestrating a melody of love that continues to play in the recesses of our hearts. It's a melody that accompanies us through the cosmic highs and lows, a constant reminder that their cosmic essence remains an active participant in the unfolding chapters of our lives.

Divine Conversations:

The realm provides a unique space for conversations that transcend the limitations of vocal expression. In the quiet moments of introspection, when the cosmic dust settles, we find ourselves engaged in a dialogue that goes beyond the audible. It's a communion of souls, where our expressions of love, gratitude, and even the unspoken apologies become cosmic whispers that resonate in the universal ether.

As we navigate the currents of life, our loved ones become our silent companions, offering guidance, solace, and occasionally, a nudge when needed. Their presence is not a passive spectatorship but an active participation in the evolution of our individual and collective narratives.

Theater of Commemorations:

In the sphere of our minds, we stage commemorations, not farewells. Birthdays, anniversaries, and significant milestones become celestial stages where we celebrate the enduring impact of their cosmic footprints on our earthly journey. These tributes are not rituals of sorrow but festivals of love, where the supreme consciousness and the earthly realms intertwine.

Our loved ones, though absent in physical form, become catalysts for moments of introspection, growth, and transformation. In the alchemy of grief, their essence transmutes into an elixir that fortifies our resilience and fuels our pursuit of soul's purpose.

So, as we traverse the realms of our existence, let us not perceive the departure of our loved ones as an end but as an expansion. They are not lost in the vastness; they have become an inseparable part of it. In our hearts and memories, they exist as constellations, casting their eternal glow upon the canvas of our lives.

In this understanding, the bonds of love transcend the limitations of time and space, becoming the celestial glue that binds us to our loved ones across the dimensions. As we gaze into the expanse, may the echoes of our loved ones resonate, reminding us that their guiding presence is not a farewell but an everlasting embrace that transcends the circle of life and death.

Rituals of Remembrance: Honoring the Tapestry of Shared Existence

In the theater of life, where each soul plays a unique role in the grand production, the departure of a loved one marks not an end but a transformation. As stardust mingles with the winds, the essence of our dear departed becomes a constellation in the vast celestial expanse of memories. To honor and remember, we embark on rituals that transcend the earthly and reach into the realms, creating a tapestry of remembrance that stretches across the cosmic fabric.

1. Celestial Candlelit Vigil: In the quietude of many nights, we kindle the flame of remembrance. Lighting a celestial candle becomes a symbolic gesture, each flicker representing a cherished moment, a shared laugh, or a tender touch. As the glow illuminates the darkness, we commune with the celestial, forging a connection that transcends earthly boundaries.

> *Example: As the candle dances with the winds, we share stories of our loved ones, allowing the warmth of the flame to symbolize the enduring glow of their presence in our lives.*

2. Commemoration Altar: Creating an altar becomes an act of devotion. Elements that hold significance—a photo, a cherished possession, or symbolic representations—are arranged with intentionality. The altar becomes a focal point for remembrance, a sacred space where all Earthly and Spiritual planes converge.

> *Example: On the altar, a celestial map marks the places our loved one dreamed of visiting, symbolizing the vastness of their aspirations that transcend the earthly realm.*

3. Stargazing Soirée: Beneath the luminaries' canopy, we gather for a stargazing soirée. Armed with knowledge, we explore the celestial tapestry, identifying constellations that mirror the essence of our departed loved ones. It becomes a conversation, where each twinkle is a reply from the other side of the cosmic veil.

> *Example: Pointing to a constellation, we share how it encapsulates the adventurous spirit of our loved one, turning the canvas into a living, breathing biography.*

4. Artistic Expression: The brush becomes a conduit between the earthly and the mystical. Engaging in art—whether painting, writing, or crafting—becomes a form of sacred expression. Each stroke is a whisper, a gesture that transcends the boundaries of the tangible, weaving our loved one's essence into the fabric of universal awareness.

> *Example: A celestial painting emerges, depicting the journey of our loved one as a magnificent traveler, navigating the galaxies of experience and leaving behind a trail of stardust.*

5. Feasts of Remembrance: In the banquet of life, we set a place for our departed loved ones. feasts of remembrance involve preparing their favorite dishes and sharing meals that once echoed with their laughter. It's a celebration of the sustenance they provided during their earthly sojourn.

> *Example: As we savor the banquet, we share anecdotes of shared meals, turning the act of eating into a communion with our departed loved ones.*

These rituals of remembrance are not mere ceremonies; they are bridges that span the realms of the tangible and intangible. In weaving the tapestry of remembrance, we transcend the limits of the earthly, inviting the essence of our departed loved ones to dance with us in the grand ballad of life. In honoring their legacy, we find solace in the truth that they are not lost but transformed, becoming eternal constellations in the boundless universe.

Whispers of the Symphony: Embracing Eternal Echoes

In the ballet of existence, where the dance of life intertwines with the celestial rhythms, the departure of our loved ones is not a finale but a transformation into the eternal echoes that resonate through the cosmic corridors of time. These echoes are the ethereal footprints left behind, the whispers of love and wisdom that continue to dance with us in the symphony of our lives. As we attune our cosmic senses to these echoes, we realize that the presence of our departed loved ones is not confined to the past but is an ever-present cosmic melody, a celestial serenade that accompanies us on the journey of healing.

1. Celestial Harmonies in Everyday Sounds: Listen closely, and you'll hear the celestial harmonies woven into the fabric of everyday sounds. The wind carries the laughter of our loved ones, the rustling leaves echo with their words of comfort, and the gentle rain becomes a lullaby. In these ordinary sounds, we discover the extraordinary symphony of eternal echoes.

Example: As the wind rustles through the trees, we feel the gentle caress of a loved one's presence, a kind reminder that they are orchestrating the unseen music around us.

2. Murmurs in Synchronicities: In the tapestry of events, synchronicities become murmurs, messages from the other side of the cosmic veil. A butterfly alighting on a windowsill, a favorite song playing on the radio – these are not mere coincidences but winks, gestures from our departed loved ones saying, "We are still here."

> *Example: Spotting a rainbow on a gloomy day becomes a promise, a technicolor bridge connecting our earthly realm to the cosmic realm where our loved ones reside.*

3. Celestial Dreams as Majestic Portals: Dreams are not just nightly wanderings of the mind; they are portals where our departed loved ones visit us. In the realm of dreams, they speak to us in the language of symbols and emotions, offering guidance, solace, and sometimes, just the cosmic warmth of their embrace.

> *Example: A dream where our loved one hands us a key which becomes a metaphor for unlocking the doors of healing and understanding in our waking lives.*

4. Footprints in Sacred Spaces: The places we shared with our departed loved ones become sanctuaries. In these sacred spaces, we feel their footprints – the resonance of shared experiences, the echo of shared laughter, and the lingering energy that transcends the earthly realm.

> *Example: Visiting a favorite spot, we feel the embrace of our loved one, turning a familiar place into a sanctuary of eternal echoes.*

5. Conversations in Intuition: The realm speaks to us through the language of intuition. The subtle nudges, the gut feelings, the moments of clarity – these are conversations, the wisdom imparted by our departed loved ones from the higher realms they now inhabit.

> *Example: Trusting our intuition becomes a synchronized movement guided by the celestial choreography of our departed loved ones.*

In embracing the eternal echoes, we transcend the linear constraints of time and space. Our departed loved ones are not confined to the past; they are companions, weaving their presence into the very fabric of our existence. As we attune our senses to the whispers of the cosmic symphony, we discover that healing is not a journey toward the absence of pain but a harmonious dance with the everlasting resonances that remind us, with every note, that our loved ones are forever with us.

Sculpting Legacies: Creative Ways to Honor and Remember

In the vast canvas of the celestial tapestry, the ones we love become constellations, their light forever embedded in the fabric of our existence. Honoring and remembering a loved one is not a ritual; it's an artistic endeavor, a sculpting of legacies in the clay of time. As we embark on this creation, we discover that the palette of remembrance is vast, filled with hues of love, laughter, and cherished moments. Here are the brushstrokes to inspire your unique masterpiece of commemoration:

1. Celestial Memory Jars: Craft a memory jar, a vessel to hold the stardust of shared moments. Fill it with notes, photographs, and tokens that encapsulate the essence of your shared journey. On special occasions or when solace is needed, open the jar, and let the memories illuminate your path. Healing, in its essence, is not about discarding the melody of memories but orchestrating them into a celestial symphony. Every laugh, every shared moment, every quirk becomes a note in this composition. Healing invites us to listen to this symphony, to let the echoes of the past serenade us with the love once shared.

> *Example: In the memory jar, a note detailing a favorite shared joke becomes a chuckle, echoing through the corridors of time.*

2. Charitable Endeavors: Transform grief into a powerful force for good by engaging in charitable endeavors that reflect your cherished one's passions. Whether it's supporting a cause dear to their heart or initiating community projects, these acts become living tributes, perpetuating the legacy of love and compassion. When faced with the devastating loss of a life partner, it is easy to become self-absorbed and withdraw from the world. However, by redirecting our focus towards helping others, we not only contribute to their well-being but also cultivate a positive mindset within ourselves. Engaging in acts of kindness and service allows us to shift our perspective and find solace in knowing that we can make a difference in someone else's life.

Giving back also provides an opportunity for personal growth and development. As we extend a helping hand to those in need, we discover hidden strengths and capabilities within ourselves. Through volunteering or supporting charitable organizations, we learn to navigate new challenges, develop problem-solving skills, and enhance our emotional intelligence. This process of self-discovery not only aids in our healing but also fuels our personal growth journey.

Furthermore, helping others allows us to develop a profound sense of empathy and compassion. By immersing ourselves in the struggles of others, we gain a deeper understanding of our own pain and grief. This increased self-awareness enables us to connect with others on a more profound level, providing support and comfort to those who are going through similar experiences. In turn, this fosters a sense of community and belonging, creating a network of individuals who can lean on each other during times of hardship.

> *Example: Establishing a scholarship in their name becomes a ripple, creating waves of positive impact in the lives of aspiring students.*

3. Stellar Stargazing Rituals: Designate a night for stargazing, a celestial rendezvous with your departed loved one. Each twinkling star becomes a vessel of their essence, a Morse code conveying messages of love. Share stories, express feelings, and let the canopy be the canvas for your connection. Healing invites us to engage in a conversation with the stars, to speak to our departed loved ones through the language of the universe. The celestial bodies become messengers, carrying our words and emotions to the intergalactic beyond. In this dialogue, we find solace, realizing that the connection persists, albeit in a different form.

> *Example: Naming a constellation after the one you care for turns the expanse into a living tribute, a monument in the night sky.*

4. Recipe Remembrances: Compile a cookbook of recipes that hold significance in your shared history. Each dish becomes a culinary constellation, a taste of the memories you crafted together. On special occasions, prepare these concoctions, savoring the flavors of love and nostalgia.

> *Example: Baking the favorite cake, you shared on anniversaries becomes a communion, a sweet ode to enduring love.*

5. Time-Traveling Through Scrapbooks: Create scrapbooks that transcend time, capturing the journey you embarked on together. Incorporate photographs, letters, and mementos, turning the scrapbook into a time-traveling vessel that transports you back to cherished moments whenever opened.

> *Example: A pressed flower from a memorable outing becomes a time capsule, preserving the essence of that special day.*

6. Celestial Art Installations: Expressing their essence through art installations. Sculptures, paintings, or digital creations become gateways, embodying the energy, love, and uniqueness of their spirit. Display these celestial artworks in places that hold significance. Picture healing as an artist's palette, where the hues of remembrance paint a canvas of shared experiences. The vibrant strokes of joy, the muted shades of sorrow—all coalesce to create a masterpiece that transcends the boundaries of time. Healing invites us to gaze upon this cosmic artwork, appreciating the beauty woven into the fabric of our journey.

> *Example: A sculpture capturing their favorite quote becomes a tangible manifestation of their wisdom and spirit.*

7. Commemorative Rituals: Establish commemorative rituals, and ceremonies that honor significant milestones or anniversaries. Light candles, play their favorite music, and engage in activities that celebrate their life and impact on your existence. Healing is not an amnesia that erases the footprints of love left behind. Instead, it is an acknowledgment that love, like stardust, becomes part of the eternal echoes in the corridors of our hearts. The truth is that the ones we love never truly depart; they reside in the perennial echoes of our thoughts, our dreams, and the embrace of our memories.

> *Example: Releasing lanterns on their birthday becomes a celestial ceremony, the ascending lights symbolizing the eternal journey of their spirit.*

In the atelier of remembrance, there are no boundaries, only the limitless canvas of creativity. Honoring and remembering a lost one is not a static task; it's a dynamic, ever-evolving masterpiece. As you weave the threads of love, laughter, and shared experiences, remember that the legacy you sculpt is as unique as the fingerprint of the one you hold dear. The tapestry of remembrance is vast and ever-expanding, and your brushstrokes contribute to the eternal beauty of the canvas.

8. Legacy of Love: Healing, in its cosmic wisdom, acknowledges that the legacy of love is not confined to the past. It is an inheritance, a guiding light that illuminates our present and shapes our future. The ones we've lost live on in the legacy of love, an eternal flame that transcends the boundaries of temporal existence.

In the atelier of remembrance, there are no boundaries, only the limitless canvas of creativity. Honoring and remembering a lost one is not a static task; it's a dynamic, ever-evolving masterpiece. As you weave the threads of love, laughter, and shared experiences, remember that the legacy you sculpt is as unique as the fingerprint of the one you hold dear. The tapestry of remembrance is vast and ever-expanding, and your brushstrokes contribute to the eternal beauty of the canvas.

CHAPTER 10

Creating a new Vision

Finding Meaning and Purpose

Rediscovering Personal Identity

Losing a spouse to cancer is an incredibly challenging experience that can leave us feeling lost and disconnected from our own personal identity. In the aftermath of such a devastating loss, it is essential to embark on a journey of rediscovering our personal identity. The following aims to provide guidance and support to those who have experienced this profound loss, offering insights on how to rebuild a sense of self and navigate the path towards personal growth and fulfillment.

One of the first steps in rediscovering personal identity is acknowledging that the loss of a spouse does not define who we are as individuals. While the pain and grief may feel overwhelming, it is important to remember that we still have our own unique qualities, passions, and dreams. By reflecting on our past, exploring our interests, and reconnecting with our values, we can begin to rebuild a sense of self that is separate from our role as a spouse.

Building a positive mindset and self-belief is a crucial aspect of rediscovering personal identity. The journey towards healing requires us to embrace self-compassion and practice self-care. It's essential to challenge negative thoughts and beliefs that may arise, replacing them with positive affirmations and empowering self-talk. Cultivating a positive mindset allows us to view our experiences as opportunities for growth, enabling us to move forward with resilience and strength.

Emotional intelligence and self-awareness play a vital role in the process of rediscovering personal identity. Grief can be a complex and overwhelming emotion, and it is important to develop emotional intelligence to navigate through it effectively. By allowing ourselves to experience and process our emotions, we can gain a deeper understanding of ourselves and our needs. This self-awareness empowers us to make conscious choices that align with our values and aspirations.

Rediscovering personal identity is a deeply personal and transformative journey. It is a time to reconnect with ourselves, explore new possibilities, and embrace personal growth. By focusing on personal development, positive mindset, and self-belief, we can navigate the challenges of loss and emerge stronger and more resilient.

By acknowledging our individuality, cultivating a positive mindset, and developing emotional intelligence, we can embark on a journey of self-discovery and growth. The power to rebuild and find fulfillment lies within us, and with the right tools and mindset, we can embrace our personal identity with strength and resilience.

Embarking on the Quest for Purpose: Navigating Life's Uncharted Territories After Loss

In the labyrinth of grief, losing a life partner to cancer can cast shadows over the once-familiar landscape of existence. The journey ahead may seem daunting, fraught with questions about the very essence of life's purpose and meaning. This serves as a compass, guiding those who have lost a beloved spouse through the uncharted territories of rebuilding, resilience, and the pursuit of a positive mindset.

1. Personal Cartography: The exploration of life's purpose is a deeply personal odyssey, a quest where the terrain varies for each soul. There's no universal map; instead, it's about becoming your own cartographer, sketching the contours of meaning with the ink of introspection. Grant yourself the liberty to wander through different landscapes, discovering the paths that resonate uniquely with your heart.

Navigational Wisdom: In the cartography of self-discovery, there are no wrong turns, only opportunities to unveil hidden vistas within.

2. The Tapestry of Individuality: Acknowledging the uniqueness of your journey is pivotal. Life's purpose is a mosaic, and each shard represents a facet of your individual experience. Harness the power of self-awareness and emotional intelligence; delve into the rich tapestry of your desires, values, and strengths. Let these threads weave the narrative of your personal significance.

Reflective Insight: As you explore the mosaic of your being, let your emotions and insights be the palette, painting strokes of understanding on the canvas of self-discovery.

3. Illuminating the Present Moment: Cultivating a positive mindset becomes the lantern guiding you through the darkness of loss. While the future may seem overwhelming, focusing on the present illuminates the possibilities for a hopeful and fulfilling tomorrow. Embrace gratitude for the enduring experiences and relationships that still grace your journey, allowing the light of appreciation to dispel the shadows of despair.

Mindful Affirmation: In the dance of now, find the rhythm of gratitude, for it is the melody that resonates with the symphony of a brighter future.

4. Personal Renaissance Through Development: The journey towards purpose intertwines with personal development, a continuous evolution fueled by curiosity and a thirst for growth. Engage in activities that nurture this metamorphosis —be it the written wisdom of books, the shared insights of workshops, or the compassionate guidance of therapy. In investing in your own well-being, you lay the foundation for resilience and self-belief.

Transformative Inquiry: What facets of personal development beckon to you, whispering promises of growth and a renewed sense of purpose?

5. Communal Spirits, Shared Odyssey: Remember, you're not a solitary voyager. Connect with fellow wayfarers who've tread similar paths, seek the comfort of friends and family, and lean on the supportive pillars of professional resources. In this shared odyssey, solace, healing, and the rediscovery of purpose become communal endeavors.

Harmonious Echo: As you navigate the complex landscapes, let the echoes of shared experiences amplify the courage to find new meaning and purpose after the profound loss of a spouse to cancer.

As you embark on this courageous quest, knowing that within the complexities of grief lies the potential for a transformative journey. Patience, self-compassion, and an open heart will be your steadfast companions as you navigate the uncharted territories of life after loss. Together, as a collective of resilient souls, we can find solace, healing, and a renewed sense of purpose, crafting a future that honors the memories of our beloved departed while embracing the boundless possibilities that lie ahead.

Forging a Path of Resilience: A Guide to Setting and Achieving Goals After Loss

In the aftermath of bidding farewell to a loved one, the terrain of life may seem vast, overwhelming, and shrouded in uncertainty. The once-sturdy foundations of your world may have crumbled, leaving you adrift in a sea of emotions. Yet, within this complexity lies a potent truth – the power to rebuild and sculpt a new path. In this journey of resilience and healing, the art of setting and achieving goals becomes a compass guiding you towards a future filled with purpose and hope.

1. Rediscovering Direction and Purpose: Setting goals isn't merely a roadmap; it's a lantern illuminating the path ahead. As you identify what you wish to achieve, a renewed sense of direction and purpose emerges. Whether it's personal growth, career aspirations, or the pursuit of newfound passions, goals focus your energy, empowering you to regain control over the narrative of your life.

Empowering Realization: Within the realm of your goals, discover the seeds of purpose that blossom into a garden of resilience.

2. Nurturing a Positive Mindset: Approach your goals as a gardener tends to delicate blooms. Cultivate a positive mindset and self-belief, recognizing the strength within to overcome obstacles. Setbacks and doubts may linger, but with a positive outlook, resilience becomes the companion guiding you steadfastly forward.

Mindful Gardening: In the garden of your mind, sow seeds of positivity, watered by the belief that you possess the strength to nurture your aspirations.

3. The Dance of Emotional Intelligence: Goal-setting becomes an intricate dance when led by emotional intelligence and self-awareness. Reflect on your emotions, discern your needs and values, and align your goals accordingly. By attuning yourself to the symphony of your emotions, the goals you set become harmonious notes in the melody of personal growth.

Reflective Choreography: Let the goal-setting reflect the emotions that compose the unique melody of your personal journey.

4. Realism and Achievability: Break your goals into smaller, manageable steps – the stepping stones leading to triumph. This not only makes your goals more attainable but allows for celebration at each small victory. Through these incremental achievements, you not only build momentum but also foster confidence and a profound sense of accomplishment.

Triumphant Symphony: Each achieved step is a note in the symphony of your resilience, composing a melody that resonates with triumph.

5. Adaptability in the Symphony of Life: Life, much like music, is unpredictable. Embrace flexibility, adapting your goals to the ever-changing melody of circumstances. Unexpected challenges and opportunities may arise, but with an open mind and adaptable spirit, you can adjust your goals while still progressing forward.

Adaptable Crescendo: In the symphony of life, allow your goals to adapt and harmonize with the ever-changing cadence, creating a melody of resilience.

6. Honoring Memory through Purpose: Setting and achieving goals is not an erasure of pain or a forgetting of a loved one. Instead, it's a poignant homage, honoring their memory by weaving purpose and resilience into the fabric of your life. You are not alone on this journey; seek the support of kindred spirits who understand and offer guidance.

Harmonious Tribute: Your journey is a symphony, each goal achieved a note that echoes with the memory of your loved one, creating a melody of hope and resilience.

Through the art of setting and achieving goals, you unearth your strength, forge a positive mindset, and cultivate a future brimming with hope and resilience. The path forward is illuminated by the goals you set, each one a testament to your unwavering spirit and your capacity to craft a fulfilling future.

Opening to New Relationships

Losing a spouse to cancer is an incredibly painful and life-altering experience. The grief, sadness, and feelings of loneliness can be overwhelming. It may seem impossible to imagine a future where you can open to new relationships, but it is important to remember that healing and finding happiness again is possible.

When we lose someone, we love, it is natural to feel a void in our lives. However, it is crucial to understand that opening up to new relationships does not mean forgetting about your late spouse or replacing them. It is about acknowledging that there is still room in your heart for love and connection with someone new. By allowing yourself to be open to the possibility of new relationships, you give yourself the opportunity to experience joy and companionship once again.

Embracing a positive mindset and self-belief is essential when navigating this new chapter of your life. Understand that you are deserving of love and happiness, even after loss. It is normal to have fears and doubts but remember that you have the strength and resilience to overcome them. Believe in yourself and your ability to create meaningful connections with others.

Developing emotional intelligence and self-awareness will also play a vital role in opening up to new relationships. Take the time to reflect on your emotions and understand how your past experiences may impact your current mindset. Be compassionate with yourself and allow yourself to grieve and heal at your own pace. Recognize any fears or insecurities that may arise and work on addressing them. By developing a deeper understanding of yourself, you can better navigate new relationships with clarity and authenticity.

Opening up to new relationships after losing a spouse to cancer is a personal journey that will vary for each individual. Some may feel ready to explore new connections sooner, while others may need more time to heal. Trust yourself and your intuition. Surround yourself with a supportive network of friends and family who can provide guidance and encouragement along the way.

Remember, you are not alone in this journey. Many others have experienced similar loss and have found hope and love once again. By opening up to new relationships, you can continue to grow, learn, and find joy in life while honoring the memory of your late spouse.

EPILOGUE

Embracing the Eternal Echoes of Love and Resilience

In the journey of life, we often face unimaginable challenges that test the limits of our strength and resilience. Losing someone we love to cancer is undoubtedly one of the most heartbreaking experiences we can endure. It leaves us shattered, forever changed, and searching for ways to navigate the daunting path of grief and healing.

But amidst the pain and sorrow, there are eternal echoes of love and resilience that can guide us through the darkest days. They are the remnants of the profound connection we shared with our loved ones, reminding us that their spirit continues to live on within us. These echoes are not fleeting, but rather, they become a constant source of strength and inspiration.

In this final chapter of "Eternal Echoes: A Guide to Resilience After Losing Someone to Cancer," we delve into the alchemy of resilience that emerges from embracing these eternal echoes. We address everyone who has lost a loved one to cancer, acknowledging the universality of grief and the power of collective healing.

Throughout this book, we have explored various aspects of grief and resilience, providing practical tools and heartfelt insights to help navigate this complex and often overwhelming process. Now, as we reach the end of this journey, it is crucial to remember that resilience is not about forgetting or moving on, but rather, it is about honoring our loved ones and finding a way to carry them with us as we continue to live.

The eternal echoes of love and resilience manifest in different ways for each individual. It could be the memories that bring us solace, the lessons learned from our loved ones' battles, or the strength we gain from connecting with others who have experienced similar losses. Whatever form they take, these echoes serve as a reminder that our journey does not end with loss but continues with purpose and meaning.

As we embrace these echoes, we begin to understand that our loved ones' legacies are not confined to their physical presence. Their impact on our lives transcends time and space, shaping our perspectives, values, and the way we choose to live. By embracing their eternal echoes, we find solace and strength in knowing that their love and spirit are forever intertwined with ours.

In conclusion, "Eternal Echoes: A Guide to Resilience After Losing Someone to Cancer" invites everyone who has lost a loved one to cancer to embark on a journey of healing and discovery. It encourages us to embrace the eternal echoes of love and resilience, allowing them to guide us through the darkest moments and inspire us to live with purpose and meaning. Though the pain of loss may never fully dissipate, we can find solace and strength in the eternal echoes that connect us to our loved ones, forever reminding us of the power of love and the indomitable spirit of the human heart.

FURTHER READING AND SUPPORTIVE RESOURCES

In the vast landscape of healing and personal development after the loss of a spouse, numerous valuable resources await discovery. Here is a curated list of books, articles, websites, and support organizations to illuminate your path toward resilience and growth.

Books:

1. "The Power of Now" by Eckhart Tolle - A guide to embracing the present moment and finding peace within.
2. "Dying to Be Me" by Anita Moorjani - An exploration of near-death experiences and the transformative power of self-love.
3. "Option B: Facing Adversity, Building Resilience, and Finding Joy" by Sheryl Sandberg and Adam Grant - A compelling exploration of resilience and finding joy in the face of adversity.
4. "The Artist's Way" by Julia Cameron - A transformative journey to unleash creativity and overcome challenges.
5. "The Grief Recovery Handbook" by John W. James and Russell Friedman - A compassionate guide to navigating grief and finding healing.

6. "The Last Lecture" by Randy Pausch-poignant exploration of life lessons delivered by a professor facing a terminal illness.

Articles:

1. "Coping with Grief and Loss" - American Psychological Association. Link
2. "The Healing Power of Art" - Psychology Today. Link
3. "Finding Hope and Healing After Loss" - Mayo Clinic. Link
4. "The Science of Positivity" - Greater Good Magazine. Link

Websites:

1. Grief.com - A comprehensive resource for grief support and education. Link
2. The Chopra Center - Explore meditation and holistic approaches to healing. Link
3. Psychology Today's Grief Therapists Directory - Find a grief therapist in your area. Link

Support Organizations:

1. **Grief Share:** A grief recovery support group where you can find help and healing for the hurt of losing a loved one. Link
2. **The Compassionate Friends:** Supporting family after a child dies. Link
3. **Hospice Foundation of America:** Providing resources for grief and loss. Link

Acknowledging Sources:

Throughout this book, I've drawn inspiration and wisdom from various sources. The stories shared reflect the diverse narratives of individuals who have embarked on journeys of healing. The insights shared are a tapestry woven from personal experiences, expert guidance, and the collective wisdom of those who have navigated similar paths.

I want to express my deepest gratitude for allowing me to be a companion on your healing journey. Your resilience, strength, and unwavering spirit have been a beacon of inspiration, reminding us of all of the incredible power within.

As you continue your journey, may the stars above guide you, the echoes of love surround you, and the dawn of each new day bring you closer to the peace you seek. You are a luminary in the vast cosmos of human experience, and your story, like the constellations, adds brilliance to the universe.

Remember, your path is as individual as your fingerprint. These resources are lanterns to illuminate your way, but the steps you take are uniquely yours. May your journey be one of resilience, growth, and, above all, self-discovery.

With heartfelt warmth and boundless encouragement,

Muriel Blanc

Printed in the USA
CPSIA information can be obtained
at www.ICGtesting.com
LVHW061243170424
777538LV00015BA/251